BEWARE OF RATTLESNAKES

OTHER BOOKS BY PETER JEFFERY

In addition to *Beware of Rattlesnakes*, Solid Ground is truly honored to have published the following titles by this precious man of God:

OPENING UP EPHESIANS: *A Study for New Christians and Young People*
This book is intended to explain and apply the book of Ephesians for those in the formative years of their Christian life. Perfect for High School and College age Sunday School classes, New Believer's Sunday School, Bible Studies or personal study, it has several challenging questions following each chapter, plus a Digging Deeper section for those eager to search the Bible more thoroughly for the riches contained within.

LIFE IN THE PSALMS: *Reflections on the Greatest Devotional Book in the World*
Peter Jeffery has walked with God for more than 50 years, and he has found great personal help from the Book of Psalms. In recent years his failing health has caused him to spend much of his time in bed reflecting upon God's faithfulness to him all his days. These words come from a man who has seen God work in mighty ways throughout his life and who desires to share his joy with others as long as he has breath.

CHAINS OF GRACE: *The Peter Jeffery Story*
Chains of Grace, the story of Peter Jeffery, is an engaging and insightful account of how God took an ordinary man (who had little knowledge of the Bible) and converted him, even though the very day he was converted, he vowed these words: 'I will never become a Christian!' Commencing his ministry in Wales, he faced challenges and difficulties in his pastorate, but learnt to trust God in all circumstances. His faithful preaching of the Bible led to many people having their lives transformed, and the knock-on effect of God's grace was often like the links of a chain, with one conversion leading to another. Peter's ministry took him to many different parts of the world, including Australia and North America. His writings have been translated into various languages, and he has over forty books in print.

BEWARE OF RATTLESNAKES

Lessons for Young People
From History, Sports and Odds & Ends

Peter Jeffery

SOLID GROUND CHRISTIAN BOOKS
BIRMINGHAM, ALABAMA USA

Solid Ground Christian Books
PO Box 660132
Vestavia Hills AL 35266
205-443-0311
mike.sgcb@gmail.com
www.solid-ground-books.com

BEWARE OF RATTLESNAKES
Lessons for Young People from History, Sports, Odds & Ends

First Solid Ground Edition – December 2013

Illustrations throughout book by Lorraine King

Cover design by Borgo Design
Contact them at borgogirl@bellsouth.net

ISBN- 978-159925-340-4

PREFACE

I have known Peter and Lorna Jeffery for more than 20 years, and have loved and appreciated Peter's writing and preaching from the very first time I was introduced to him. It was my distinct privilege to be the first American minister to invite him to the USA and his ministry here continued as long as his health permitted him to travel. Wherever Peter ministered the people heard him gladly. His teaching was always simple and yet powerful. Among his many gifts his ability to illustrate hard truths with memorable stories topped the list.

It is a great privilege to assist my older brother in getting this precious book into the hands of young people all over the world. My own grandchildren will be among the very first ones to read these 52 chapters drawn from history, sports and odds & ends. While some of the sports are not as familiar to those in the United States, Peter explains them in a way that will still get the vital message into their minds and hearts.

For Peter the story or the illustration is not an end but simply the means to an end. The goal is always the same: the glory of God and the good of the souls of men, women, boys and girls. He has a passion for the lost and his burden can be seen and felt on every page. He is an avid student of the history of revival and he longs to see the arm of God extended in the salvation of lost and ruined souls.

While this book was written with young people in mind it is appropriate for every one of every age. If this is your first time reading a Peter Jeffery book you are in for a treat. If you are a fan of Peter already you will not be disappointed. May the God of all grace smile upon this humble work to His glory.

Michael A. Gaydosh, the Publisher

A WORD ABOUT THE AUTHOR

Peter Jeffery was born in 1937. In 1955, at the age of 17, he became a Christian—in spite of the fact that the very day he was converted he vowed these words, "I will never become a Christian!" Peter married his high school sweetheart, Lorna, at age 21 and they had their first child at age 23. Nine days later the baby died of Spina bifida. Though Peter had been preaching since he was 18, this incident was used by God to call Peter into His service.

Peter was ordained to the ministry in 1963 at age 25 and served as the Minister at Ebenezer Congregational Church in Cwmbran, Wales. In 1972 he accepted a call to Rugby Evangelical Free Church where he ministered until 1986. In 1986 Peter went to Bethlehem Evangelical Church. There he ministered faithfully until 1994. Since 1994 Peter has had an itinerant ministry of preaching and evangelism allowing him to preach at churches and conferences in Wales, England, Scotland, Ireland, Australia, Spain, and the U.S.A.

Peter Jeffery, now retired, has been preaching for more than 50 years. His life work stands as a testimony that anointed expository preaching is not a thing of the past. Heavily influenced by Charles Spurgeon and Dr. D. Martyn Lloyd-Jones, he displays the same seriousness about the need of proclaiming the truths of the Bible.

Jeffrey has written over forty books, which have been translated into many languages. Many of his works focus on new Christians, the foundations of faith, evangelism and salvation.

TABLE OF CONTENTS

1

KING CANUTE

Canute was king of England from 1016 to 1035. He was also king of Denmark, Norway and parts of Sweden, so this was quite a remarkable man. His courtiers thought very highly of him and were always praising Canute and telling him that there was nothing he could not do. But the king was not dull enough to believe all the exaggerated compliments and he decided to teach his friends a lesson.

He commanded them to take his chair on to the beach when the tide was coming in, sitting in the chair he then commanded the water to stop, but of course it did not and he and his courtiers got wet feet. But the lesson was learned. "Well, my friends," Canute said, "it seems I do not have quite so much power as you would have me believe. Perhaps you have learned something today. Perhaps now you will remember there is only one King who is all-powerful, and it is he who rules the sea, and holds the ocean in the hollow of his hand. I suggest you reserve your praises for him."

King Canute was a Christian and he realized that only God was able to do all things. There is an incident in the New Testament when Jesus commanded the wind to stop blowing and the sea to stop raging and both wind and sea obeyed him. There is nothing impossible for Jesus because he is God. What a great God we have and we should reserve our praises for him.

Stop for a moment and think of all the things God has done for you. Then consider the beauty of this world that God has placed us in. The trees, the mountains, the sea and all of creation we have to enjoy. And what about your family and all who love you and care for you. Above all think about Jesus and your salvation. We have a great deal to praise God for.

Canute said that God is all powerful and he was right. The God of the Bible is a God of varied and limitless power and it is impossible to compare with this power the greatest achievements of the mightiest men. Have you ever stood in a great cathedral and admired the huge structure and vast arches? You may ask, 'who made this?' When you look in the guidebook you see it took thousands of men over a hundred years to construct that building. Then go outside and look at the sky, the stars and the moon; see the glory of the mountains and the sea, and ask, 'who made all this?' The answer is, God did and did it alone and did it in a moment. He said, 'Let there be -' and there was. That is the power of God.

I remember in the 1950s seeing the film *The Ten Commandments* and being particularly impressed with the scene of the opening of the Red Sea. I thought it was very clever; it looked so real. Then I suddenly thought, God actually did it. No trick camera work, but omnipotence parted those waters. That is real power.

The reality of God's power seems to confuse men. They do not believe it and dismiss the miracles of the Bible as myth. It is impossible, they say. But impossible to whom? To men, to politicians, to scientists, yes, but not to God. We must not limit God by our limitations.

Another difficulty men have with divine omnipotence is that they misinterpret it. You do not have to read the Bible for very long to discover the difference in outlook between the men of Scripture and modern man. Where those men saw God, we see the laws of nature. We have reduced the omnipotent God to a set of laws and forget that what we see in nature is simply the paths that God's power and wisdom take.

Key verse	Exodus 14:13-14
Main application	Nothing is impossible with God
Key Theme	Only God is almighty
The 'Story'	God rules over all
Application	You can depend upon God when all else seems hopeless

2

ROBERT THE BRUCE

King Robert the Bruce I was born in 1274 and in 1306 he was crowned King of Scotland and tried to free Scotland from the English enemy. After being defeated at a battle, Bruce escaped and found a hideout in a cave. Hiding in a cave for three months, Bruce was at the lowest point of his life. He thought about leaving the country and never coming back.

Suddenly his eye was caught by a spider—the creature was hanging by a long silvery thread from one of the wooden beams above his head, and trying to swing itself to another beam. The spider tried again and again, failing every time. Six times, counted Robert, the spider tried and failed. 'Six times,' thought Robert to himself, 'have I fought against the English and failed.'

Robert looked at the spider more intently. 'Now if this spider fails again on the seventh attempt, I too shall give up the fight for Scotland. But if it succeeds, I shall try again.' The spider, as though aware of Robert's thought, swung itself again with all its tiny strength—and finally, on the seventh attempt, it succeeded. It swung on to the beam it had been trying to reach, and fastened its thread, thus stretching the first line of the web it was trying to weave.

Whether this old legend is true or not it is certainly true that Robert threw off his despair and grief, and determined to continue his fight against the English. He fought against the English for the next eight years, defeating them and finally driving them out of Scotland in 1314, at the Battle of Bannockburn.

It is very easy to give in when things get difficult. The history of Christianity is full of difficult times when it seemed that the church could never survive. During the New Testament time everything was against the Christians. They were forbidden to preach the gospel and were killed if they did. But like Robert the Bruce they kept on and it was not a spider that encouraged them but the promises of God in the Bible that he would never leave them or forsake them.

He is still the same God and his promises still hold true. So trust God to give you the victory just as he has done for Christians in the past, and even though God does not always give the victory in the way we expect, he will never fail us.

About the year 155 a very old Christian named Polycarp was captured by the Roman rulers and they demanded that he say that Caesar, the emperor, was god. If he did not he would be killed. Polycarp answered them, 'Eighty six years have I served Christ and he has done me no wrong: how can I then blaspheme my King who has saved me?' He was killed but he knew a great victory.

Very often in the life of the church the best things happen at the least expected times. The story is told of a country church in Wales during the 1859 revival. On a particular Sunday, they had no recognized preacher in the pulpit. Great things were happening in the land and thousands were coming to faith in Christ, but on this Sunday no-one was expecting much blessing. In the prayer meeting before the service one man prayed, 'Lord, you know we have no great preacher here today.' He went on to describe some preachers as like a beautiful suit of clothes, but their preacher that day was just a tatty old sleeve.

To everyone's surprise, the preacher was mightily used by God that day and many were saved. It was recognized that though the preacher was only a tatty old sleeve, God's arm had filled the sleeve and great blessing flowed.

Maybe your pastor is not much of a preacher. Perhaps you are tempted to talk rather disparagingly about his ministry, but remember the tatty old sleeve and what God can do. Pray that God's arm will fill the sleeve in your church. The man God used in a most remarkable way in Wales during the 1859 revival was a Presbyterian minister named David Morgan. He had exercised a very ordinary ministry for a number of years, but he said that one night he went to bed like a lamb and woke up like a lion. The power of the Holy Spirit had come upon him.

Pray earnestly for your minister that the same God-given power may come upon his preaching.

Key Verse	Proverbs 3:5-6
Main application	Don't give up
Key Theme	The tatty old sleeve can become invincible
The Story	The story of Polycarp
Application	Trust God at all times

3

GEORGE WASHINGTON

George Washington was the first president of America. He was elected in 1789, and again in the 1792 election; he remains the only president to receive 100% of the electoral votes. Clearly he was a good man and the story is told of an incident when he was 6 years old that showed the sort of man he was to become.

When George was about six years old, he was given an axe of which, like most little boys, he was extremely fond. He went about chopping everything that came his way.

One day, as he wandered about the garden amusing himself by hacking his mother's pea sticks, he found a beautiful, young English cherry tree, of which his father was most proud. He tried the edge of his axe on the trunk of the tree and barked it so that it died.

Sometime after this, his father discovered what had happened to his favorite tree. He came into the house in great anger, and demanded to know who the person was who had cut away the bark. Nobody could tell him anything about it.

Just then George, with his little axe, came into the room.

"George," said his father, "do you know who has killed my beautiful little cherry tree yonder in the garden? I would not have taken five guineas for it!"

This was a hard question to answer, and for a moment George was staggered by it, but quickly recovering himself he cried:

"I cannot tell a lie, father, you know I cannot tell a lie! I did cut it with my little axe."

The anger died out of his father's face, and taking the boy tenderly in his arms, he said:

"My son, that you should not be afraid to tell the truth is more to me than a thousand trees! Yes—though they were blossomed with silver and had leaves of the purest gold!"

Why was it that young George could not tell a lie? Many 6 year olds would not have hesitated to blame their sister or the boy next door. What would you have done? It is very easy to lie especially if it gets you out of trouble. God hates lies. One of the Ten Commandments he gave us to live by says, 'You shall not give false testimony against your neighbor," which means that we are not to lie. Jesus said, 'Simply let your 'Yes' be 'Yes,' and your 'No,' 'No'; anything beyond this comes from the evil one'.

The truth is very important to God and it ought to be important to us. Very often today truth is alright if it does not cost too much. It has become a matter of convenience. That is all the more reason why Christians should cherish it very highly and not just in theory but in practice. Christians are meant to be different and the difference should be obvious.

When I was a student in college, I spent two summers working for a local council, cutting grass in a cemetery. The man in charge of the cemetery had a strange aversion to anything Christian and lost no opportunity to attack my Christian faith.

One day as we were working together, he pointed to a man walking through the cemetery and said, 'There's a man who was ruined by Christianity.' He went on to explain that during the Second World War that man was deeply involved in the local 'black market'. In the war years everyone had ration books; everything was in short supply and certain goods were virtually impossible to obtain. But the 'black market' men could get you anything—at a highly-inflated price. I was told that this man was making a fortune selling goods on the 'black market'. 'He was raking it in,' said my foreman, 'but then he got converted and gave it all up. Christianity ruined him.'

What a marvelous, even though unintentional, testimony to the power of the gospel! Paul says that when we become Christians, we become new creatures; old things pass away, all things become new. Christianity ruins us for dishonesty and greed. It breaks the power of sin. Christ gives us a new life with new ambitions, new desires, new standards. It ruins us for sin.

Key Verse/Passage	Philippians 4:8
Main Application	Telling lies is never right
Key themes	The truth can be hard but is always right
The 'Story'	George Washington and the cherry tree
Application	The Christian life can be costly

4

TEDDY ROOSEVELT

Roosevelt was the 26th president of the USA from 1901 to 1909. He is remembered for many things but perhaps the strangest is for the teddy bear.

Ever the sportsman, TR was hunting in Mississippi during his first term in office. It had been a bad day on the trail, and Roosevelt's Mississippi hosts were disturbed by the fact that the President's trip had been spoiled by a lack of animals. A few members of the hunting party caught a small bear cub, and invited TR, as the guest of honor, to take the "trophy". Roosevelt refused, stating that it simply would not be sporting to kill the cub. Newspapers nationwide publicized the event.

The American people were thrilled by the story and soon one toy maker had made a cuddly toy bear and called it Teddy's bear. Right up to the present time very few children have grown up without a teddy bear.

What would you like to be remembered for? Perhaps you think you will never do anything worthwhile remembering. That may be true but you never know.

Mary Jones was from a poor family, the daughter of a weaver, who lived at the foot of Cader Idris, near Dolgellau. She was born in December 1784. Her parents were devout Calvinistic Methodists, and she herself professed the Christian faith at eight years of age. Having learned to read in the circulating schools organized by Thomas Charles, it became her burning desire to possess a Bible of her own. The nearest copy was at a farm two miles distant from her little cottage, and there was no copy on sale nearer than Bala—25 miles away; and it was not certain that a copy could be obtained there. Welsh Bibles were scarce in those days. Having saved for six years until she had enough money to pay for a copy, she started one morning in 1800 for Bala, and walked the 25 miles, barefoot as usual, to obtain a copy from the Rev. Charles, the only individual with Bibles for sale in the area. According to one version of the story, Mr. Charles told her that all of the copies which he had received were sold or already spoken for. Mary was so upset that Charles spared her one of the copies already promised to another. In another version, she had to wait two days for a supply of Bibles to arrive, and was able to purchase a copy for herself and two other copies for members of her family. According to tradition, it was the impression that this visit by Mary Jones left upon him that led Charles to propose to the Council of the Religious Tract Society to form a Society to supply Wales with Bibles.

Mary Jones just wanted a Bible but that wish causes us to remember her today.

In the 19th century in Scotland there was a great preacher named Robert Murray M'Cheyne. He was a remarkable man but sadly he died when he was only twenty seven. He prayed one day that the Lord would make him as holy as it was possible for a sinner to be. That's a great ambition for any Christian. We spend so much time excusing our sin and lamenting that we are so sinful. But the truth is that we are as holy as we want to be.

Christians say sometimes when they have sinned, 'I could not help it. I tried not to do it, but the temptation was too great.'

How does this square with the teaching of Romans 6 that we are dead to sin and that the slavery of sin finished the moment we were saved? Quite simply, the above excuse cannot be justified biblically. Sin is no longer our master, therefore it cannot compel us to do anything. There is a difference between temptation and compulsion. To the temptation we can say 'yes' or 'no'. Compulsion does not give us that choice.

The Christian is not a slave to sin and therefore not under sin's compulsion. Sin can tempt us, but it cannot force us. We are in Christ and therefore dead to sin's slavery.

Key Verse/Passage	1 Corinthians 10:13
Main Application	Mary Jones's desire for a Bible
Key themes	Small things can be important
The 'Story'	What does a Teddy Bear remind you of?
Application	God is faithful

5

GEORGE W. BUSH

George W. Bush was president of the USA from 2001 to 2009. One day he was visiting a marine training fort where he was to meet with the families of those who had recently lost their loved ones in the war. It was arranged for a few of the young marines to meet Mr. Bush at a luncheon held in his honor.

One of these marines said to the President, "May I say something to you?"

"Yes", was the reply.

The young marine said, "My family and I pray for you every day."

Mr. Bush drew near the young marine, put his arm around him and told him, "That is the best thing you can do for your President. Please thank your family for me."

Later, after lunch was over, on preparing to meet with those grieving families, as the President passed by that young marine he stopped and said to him, "Remember to thank your family for me."

President Bush knew that the job he had was way beyond the natural abilities of any man. He needed the prayers of the American people. The Bible commands us to pray for those who rule over us and we ought to do so every day. But whether we are presidents or little no-bodies we all need prayer. Do you have people who pray for you? Family and friends, a Sunday

School teacher or pastor, we should value these folk above all else. And do you pray for some friends? Do you ask God to look after them and bless them?

You can never be too young to learn the value of prayer. It is not something just for older Christians. Learn to pray for yourself and for others. But don't let your prayers be vague like, 'God bless the missionaries.' Find out about some particular missionary, read his prayer letters that your parents probably receive and pray for him by name.

Prayer is not easy and sometimes we get lost for words but keep at it because that is what God wants you to do.

Experiencing difficulty in prayer is common to all Christians. You find it difficult to concentrate; you find your mind wandering; you even find yourself thinking evil thoughts. You may read of Christians spending four or five hours in prayer, and the devil tells you to compare that to your five or ten minutes in prayer—and that makes you despair of prayer altogether. But you must not do so. Do not let the devil deceive you. If you are a young Christian now, in twenty years' time you will still be having the same problems. It has nothing to do with age, and little to do with experience. It is part and parcel of the constant battle we have with the flesh and the devil.

So often our whole concept of prayer is unbiblical. We think that if prayer is difficult, it must be useless or wrong. But the words that Paul uses to describe prayer are 'wrestling' (Colossians 4:12) and 'striving' (Romans 15:30 AV). He realized that there was a great battle going on. And the Christian is never so much in the front line of the battle as when he is praying. Often these difficulties arise before we even get to our knees. We find it difficult to find a suitable time to pray, and it is easy then to fall into the trap of fitting it in when it is convenient. If you do that, do not be surprised to find that it is not being 'fitted in' very much at all. The devil will see to that. I am not trying to depress you by mentioning all these problems. If you really are a Christian you will have discovered most of them already. The question is, 'How do we deal with them?'

Fix a regular time for prayer and stick to it; if your thoughts begin to wander, pray audibly instead of silently; do not give in, but keep on striving.

Key Verse/Passage	James 5:16-17
Main Application	Pray without ceasing
Key themes	There is nothing more important than prayer
The 'Story'	The young marine's witness
Application	No matter how great you are you need prayer

6

GELERT

Gelert was neither a king nor a president. He was a dog, but he belonged to Llewellyn the Great, Prince of Wales. Just outside of Beddgelert you can see today the grave of Gelert and carved on the stone is the following...

"In the 13th century Llewellyn, prince of North Wales, had a palace at Beddgelert. One day he went hunting without Gelert, "The Faithful Hound", who was unaccountably absent. On Llewellyn's return the truant, stained and smeared with blood, joyfully sprang to meet his master. The prince alarmed hastened to find his son, and saw the infant's cot empty, the bedclothes and floor covered with blood.

The frantic father plunged his sword into the hound's side, thinking it had killed his heir. The dog's dying yell was answered by a child's cry. Llewellyn searched and discovered his boy unharmed, but nearby lay the body of a mighty wolf which Gelert had slain. The prince filled with remorse is said never to have smiled again. He buried Gelert here".

It's an amazing story of what can happen when we jump too quickly to conclusions. Llewellyn made a terrible mistake by not stopping to find out the facts. It is very easily done and can cause untold anguish and pain. Many people do this with Jesus. They think of Jesus as a great teacher or a marvelous example for us to live up to, but he is much more than that. Jesus is the Son of God. He is the one God sent into this world to be our Savior. There is no one like Jesus.

It is a fatal mistake to think of Jesus as anything less because then we do not seek him to forgive us our sins. The full facts about Jesus we find in the Bible.

There is a story in Joshua 22 of when the Israelites came to a hasty conclusion and nearly started a civil war. Read the chapter for yourself.

If the two and a half tribes were wrong in building the altar, then so too were the rest of the Israelites. They heard about the altar and immediately jumped to the wrong conclusion. Their thinking was that an altar could only mean one thing, and that was sacrifice. They knew that sacrifice outside of God's ordained place was sin; therefore this was sinful.

Their brethren's action may have been stupid but it was not sinful. How often are we caught out like this? We conclude that there can be only one explanation for a certain action, but we are wrong and there is another explanation. The sad thing is that the Israelites were quick to attribute the worst possible motives to the very brethren upon whom only very recently they had heaped praise. And in no time they were prepared to go to war with them.

Are we like this? What do you do when you hear that a Christian whom you have known and respected has done or said some terrible thing? Do you immediately accept what you hear to be the truth, or do you refuse to believe it until you have spoken to that Christian and heard his explanation? How often do we say to someone, 'I heard such and such a thing about Mr. X. I don't know if it is true, but. .. '? If we do not know whether it is true then we ought to be quiet. Many a fine Christian has had his reputation ruined by such gossip. Many a faithful pastor's ministry has been seriously undermined by such irresponsible talk.

Innocent actions can be misconstrued, exaggerated and blown up out of all proportion. Sometimes we misrepresent an action of a fellow believer because we do not like that person and are only too glad for an opportunity to criticize. That is evil and wicked. Sometimes we misrepresent an action because we disagree with it. That is dishonest because the motives can be right even when the action is wrong.

The Israelites were too quick to misconstrue and much too quick to be ready to fight, but we must pay tribute to them that before they did anything they sent representatives to talk with their brethren. When they came face to face and talked the whole business through the matter was peacefully resolved.

Key Verse/Passage	2 Peter 2:10-12
Main Application	Don't jump to conclusions
Key themes	Think before you act
The 'Story'	Gelert
Application	Gossip has ruined many a church

7

MANASSEH

Manasseh was king of Judah for 55 years and he has been described as the most wicked man who ever lived. That is is some title but Manasseh deserved it. His father Hezekiah was a good king but he turned against all that his father stood for. He forbad the people to worship God and introduced evil religion to Judah. The Bible says that Manasseh, 'led them astray, so that they did more evil than the pagan nations who lived around them.'

Human sacrifice of children was a feature of this evil and Manasseh filled Jerusalem with blood from one end to the other. The temple, built to worship God, was used to worship the stars and the king destroyed all the copies of the Bible he could find.

God was angry with Manasseh but it seemed that the king was getting away with all his evil deeds. Then God brought the king of Assyria to fight against Judah and take Manasseh in chains back to Babylon. In his prison cell Manasseh thought of all the evil he had done and he repented, he was very sorry, and asked God to forgive him.

Would you forgive a man like Manasseh? Would you think that he deserved all that was coming to him? If he had sacrificed someone you loved would you hear his cry for mercy? Perhaps we would not, but God did and gave him complete forgiveness.

We all ought to be grateful that it is God we have to deal with and not each other. We can find forgiveness very difficult, but God can forgive all sin because of what Jesus did on the cross. We are not so evil as Manasseh but our sin is very real and God is just as angry with that as he was with the king's sin. But God can do for us what he did for evil Manasseh. If we confess our sin to him and ask for forgiveness, God in his mercy will grant it. Jesus died on the cross to make this possible.

Salvation is more than just the forgiveness of sin. Thank God there is forgiveness for guilty sinners; but the gospel offers us more than that.

It is not unusual from time to time to hear that the ruler of a country on some great national occasion offers an amnesty to certain convicted criminals. Their sentences are reduced and they are set free. That is not an everyday occurrence but it is not unheard of. But what is never heard of is that the Queen, after granting the amnesty, should then stand at the gates of the gaol to welcome the forgiven criminals as they come to freedom—and then tell them that, as well as granting them freedom, she now wants them to come and live at Buckingham Palace, where she will treat them like one of the family. The love and care she shows to Charles, Anne, Andrew and Edward she will now show to them.

That is unheard of and is so impossible that it seems ridiculous even to think of it. But that is exactly what God does when he saves guilty sinners. He pardons all their sin—past, present and future—but more than that, he adopts them into his family. He makes them joint heirs with Christ of all the riches of heaven. He becomes their Father and they, because of adoption, are able to call him Father.

That is the glorious salvation that we have in the Lord Jesus Christ. It is far, far more than forgiveness.

Key Verse/Passage	1 John 1: 9
Main Point	Plenteous grace with thee is found
Key themes	Forgiveness for all sin
The 'Story'	Manasseh
Application	There is no one too sinful to be saved

8

JOSIAH

Josiah was Manasseh's grandson and he became king of Judah when he was only eight years old. He was completely different to his grandfather and wanted to follow God, but he did not know how to do this. When he was 16 years old he began to seek after God with great seriousness, and when he was 20 he led a reform in the land that saw all the idols thrown out.

While they were repairing the temple Josiah's men found, probably in a pile of rubbish in some dark corner, a copy of God's Law that had been given to Moses. They brought the book to the king and read it to him. Remember now that for years Josiah had wanted to know more of God but this was not easy because of what his grandfather had done.

As soon as the king heard the words of God's book he realized that this was what he had been looking for. The book showed him his sin and what God required from him. It was not pleasant to read this and Josiah said, 'Great is the Lord's anger that is poured out on us because our father's have not kept the word of the Lord; they have not acted in accordance with all that is written in this book'. From that moment Josiah sought to follow God in the way God wanted.

If you want to follow God then you to must come to read God's word and see there what it is that he wants from you.

HOW SHOULD WE USE THE BIBLE?
We will never use the Bible effectively unless we love it. The Psalmist set the right example for us when he said, 'Oh, how I

love your law' (119:97). If we truly believe that the Bible is the word of God then we ought to love and treasure it. Love is more than admiration and respect. Why did William Tyndale give his life so that we could have the Scriptures in English? It was not because he admired this amazing book but because he loved it.

Such a love will determine how we use the Bible. If like the psalmist we can say, 'Oh, how I love your law!', then the next part of the verse will be inevitable—'I meditate on it all day long.'

Several years ago I went to preach at a church in Spain and took two young men from my church with me. One fell in love with a girl in the Spanish church. Their love for each other was obvious but language was a problem. He could not speak Spanish and she could not speak English. As soon as we returned to England this young man enrolled in night classes to learn to speak Spanish. He had no interest in Spanish before, but now he loved this girl and desired to express his love in words she could understand. Love will always motivate action and will enable the action not to be a burden but a delight. If we love God's word then we will give time to meditate upon it, not occasionally when we feel like it, but day and night (Psalm 1:1-2).

The regular daily use of the Bible is crucial. If as the Apostle Peter says, the Bible is spiritual food for our soul and promotes spiritual growth, then daily feeding is obviously necessary. One of the prime hindrances to spiritual growth is indwelling sin, and God's answer to this is Scripture—'I have hidden your word in my heart that I might not sin against you' (Psalm 119:11). Mediation implies thought, time and effort. It is quite the opposite to a casual dipping into Scripture. The person who is mediating is serious and not in a hurry. You will never benefit much from a reading of the Bible that is too quick and shallow.

No real Christian would deny the need for a daily use of Scripture, but very often the spirit is willing and the flesh is weak. How many times we make good resolutions to be more diligent in our

Bible study only to revert back to our old ways in a few weeks. So how do we combat this? Start by loving God's word, if you do this you are half way there. But you need also to recognize that there are two areas of Bible use—reading and studying. Make sure that both these are a daily part of your life.

Key Verse/Passage	Psalm 119:97-104
Main Point	Trust and obey
Key themes	Psalm 119:9-11
The 'Story'	Losing and finding the Book
Application	Psalm 119:33- 40

9

MARY TUDOR

Mary was Queen of England from 1553 until 1558. She was the daughter of Henry VIII and Catherine of Aragon. Unlike her father she was a devout Roman Catholic and set about making England a Catholic land. This involved a persecution of Protestants for which she earned the name *Bloody Mary*. It was during this period that Hugh Latimer, Nicholas Ridley and Thomas Cranmer were burnt at the stake.

For over 200 years the French city of Calais had been ruled by England and during Mary's reign it was taken back by the French. This deeply upset the queen and she said *'when I am dead you will find Calais written on my heart'*. She meant that it was the biggest disappointment of her life and it hurt her greatly.

Do you have anything written on your heart like that? Some happening that you cannot forget and the thought of it upsets you. Or it may be something very pleasant and the memory fills you with joy. It is written on your heart forever. The hymn-writer Charles Wesley had something he could never forget. A year after he was converted he wrote a hymn to commemorate his salvation. It was 'O for a thousand tongues to sing my great redeemers praise'. May 21st 1738 was a day he could never forget. On that day he ceased to be an enemy of God and became a child of God.

He wrote, 'I felt a violent opposition and reluctance to believe,' he goes on to report, 'yet still the Spirit of God strove with my own and evil spirit, till by degrees he chased away the darkness of my unbelief. I found myself convinced, I knew not how nor when; and immediately fell to intercession.'

That evening he wrote, 'I now found myself at peace with God, and rejoiced in hope of loving Christ. My temper for the rest of the day was mistrust of my own great, but before unknown weakness. I saw that by faith I stood; by the continual support of faith, which kept me from falling, though of myself I am ever sinking into sin. I want to be still sensible of my own weakness ... yet confident of Christ's protection.'

The great difference between Mary Tudor and Charles Wesley was that he was a Christian and she was not. He knew Jesus as his Savior and all she knew was religion. Being a Christian is far more than being religious. It brings us into a personal relationship with the Lord Jesus Christ. Wesley beautifully describes this in the words of the hymn mentioned above.

1. O for a thousand tongues to sing
My dear Redeemer's praise!
The glories of my God and King,
The triumphs of His grace.

2. My gracious Master, and my God,
Assist me to proclaim,
To spread through all the earth abroad
The honors of Thy name.

3. Jesus, the name that charms our fears,
That bids our sorrows cease;
'Tis music in the sinner's ears,
'Tis life, and health, and peace!

4. He breaks the power of cancell'd sin,
He sets the prisoner free;
His blood can make the foulest clean,
His blood avail'd for me.

Nicodemus was a very religious man. In fact, Jesus called him 'the teacher of Israel' and yet with all of his sincerity our Lord told him that unless he was born again he would never see nor enter the kingdom of God. Nicodemus was sincere, but he was unsaved. Read the opening verses of John 3 and you will see that religion is not enough.

Gladly the story of Nicodemus does not end in John 3. Later in John 7:45-52 he speaks up for Jesus in the midst of the other religious leaders and receives a rebuke from them. And then in John 19:38-40 we see this man one last time as he steps out of the dark with Joseph of Arimathea to accept the body of Jesus from the cross and place him in the tomb. When all of the others fled for fear of the Jews, these men stepped forward to identify themselves with the crucified Savior. Three days later they were rewarded for their service when Jesus rose from the dead. What a glorious day.

Key Verse/Passage	John 3:3
Main Point	Religion is not enough
Key themes	The need for new life in Christ
The 'Story'	Nicodemus, sincere but unsaved
Application	The full riches of grace

10

HENRY VIII

Henry VIII was a remarkable man and very talented. He spoke four languages, wrote poetry and knew a lot about religion. But he was a very cruel man and killed anyone who disagreed with him. He was a very big man especially towards the end of his life and in order to be impressive in battle he had a special suit of armor made. This can still be seen today in Windsor Castle. The claim was that wearing this armor he was invulnerable. Could you imagine Henry charging into battle with his helmet on and carrying his sword and shield, but still wearing his night-shirt. Of course not, that would be ridiculous. Yet many Christians do exactly that.

Being a Christian is not easy. Whether you are 10 years old or 50 you will find that you are in a spiritual battle. Left to yourself you would not last ten minutes but you are not on your own. Your own strength is not good enough, you need the strength which God supplies.

I was sitting on the grass with my five year old grandson watching the birds in the sky. I said to him why can't we fly like the birds? Without a moment's hesitation he said, 'Because we do not have batteries.' All his toys worked on batteries. That is where they got their power from, so to him the answer was obvious. Many Christians are like that. They see great problems and feel powerless to cope with them. They are wrong. We don't have batteries, but we do have the power of the Holy Spirit. Your strength is derived from Christ. It is only through Him that you became a conqueror; in and of yourself you are no match for Satan.

Just as Henry VIII had specially made armor so does every believer. The armor is available, but it has to be put on. It will not put itself on, and God will not put it on for us. Paul is very definite in Ephesians 6:11, and again in verse 13. The command is clear and crisp: 'Put on the full armor of God'. This is a matter of discipline and, of course, of obedience.

No army can function without discipline. Battles are won and lost not so much by great deeds of bravery on the part of one or two, but by the planning and strategy of the generals and the discipline of the soldiers in carrying it out. Consequently, almost the first thing a recruit is taught when he joins the army is discipline. In basic training he will spend a great deal of time learning to obey. Hours are spent on the parade square, in what is known as 'square-bashing'. Quick march, right turn, left turn, about turn, slope arms, present arms, order arms–the commands come quick and fast, until they are obeyed without hesitation. In any war, discipline can be a matter of life and death. During the Second World War, when enemy planes were approaching, the warning siren sounded, and the discipline of reacting immediately by rushing to the air-raid shelter saved many lives. The same discipline caused everyone to carry a gas-mask at all times. If there were an attack of gas bombs, what use would this protection be if you did not have it with you?

If this is true when fighting flesh and blood, how much more so when fighting the enemy described in verse 12! Paul tells Timothy that without discipline there is no hope of victory (1 Timothy 4:7,8). He urges him, 'train yourself to be godly'. Are you doing that? The athlete in his physical training needs a great deal of discipline, and so does the Christian, both in preparing for the battle and indeed throughout the battle.

We will not stand in the battle simply because we are saved; neither will you stand merely by taking a great interest in the truth, or in faith, or in prayer. You need them *ALL:* not truth *or* faith *or* prayer, but truth *and* faith *and* prayer. There are

Christians who are unshakeable on the truth of Scripture, but they are not much use as soldiers of the Lord because they do not know the true place and value of prayer. The opposite can also be true. It is possible to put a strong emphasis on prayer and give much time to it, and yet to accomplish little or nothing in the battle. The reason is that because such people neglect Scripture, they are easily deceived by the wiles of Satan. The only way to endure is with the whole armor on.

Our strength comes from God and God alone, and we need the armor He provides?

Key Verse/Passage	Ephesians 6:13
Main Point	The spiritual battle
Key themes	Spiritual discipline
The 'Story'	Going into battle
Application	Victory is assured but it's not easy

11

KING EDWARD I and the PRINCE OF WALES

Edward I of England wanted to please his Welsh subjects. Obviously the Welsh did not like being ruled by the English and they needed to be kept happy. So Edward promised them a prince who was born in Wales and spoke no English. As far as the Welsh were concerned this was good and they looked forward to the coming of the prince. He was born at Caernarfon on April 25 in 1284. True to the promise of Edward the new prince spoke not a word of English. In fact being as he was a new born baby he spoke nothing at all. Edward had not actually lied to the Welsh people but he had tricked them completely. Just how successful the trick was in the long run is difficult to see, but you can be sure that the people of Wales never believed the king again.

Edward probably thought he was very clever, but lies are never clever and they are never right. The ninth commandment is very clear that we are not to tell lies. It is argued that not all lies are covered by the ninth commandment. Circumstances make cases; so, for instance, is it so terrible to tell a dying man that he will recover from his illness? Is not this a kindness rather than a sin? So we talk of harmless white lies, and there is an element of truth in this reasoning, but none the less it is a very dangerous path for a Christian to walk. Who decides what is harmless and what is not?

Does any circumstance justify sin? And no one can doubt that lying is sin. In Rahab's circumstances in Joshua 2 it could be argued that she was forced either to tell a lie or to betray the spies, which meant that they would be killed. She was

30

confronted with a dilemma in which she had to choose between the lesser of two evils and we would all have to sympathize with her. But surely that is an argument that takes no account of God. Had Rahab kept silent and refused to say anything, or had she even told the truth, was God unable to protect his servants? Do we believe that God needs a violation of his own laws to bring about his will and purpose?

The New Testament emphasizes Rahab's faith and ignores her lie. Is this because the New Testament writers recognized that the faith of this woman was still immature? She knew little of the ways of the Lord and acted according to the light she had. If we were honest, we would have to admit that in a similar situation we would probably have done the same thing. Without the restraining hand of God the strongest of us are mere weaklings, and therefore none of us is in any position to point a finger at Rahab, but neither is any justified in condoning her action. Rahab is not to be used as an excuse to lie. What we ought to do is pray that the Lord would keep us from such situations. We see in Scripture several situations in which we could be tempted to lie. Rahab lied to protect others. Peter, in the courtyard, lied to avoid trouble for himself. Ananias and Sapphira lied to impress others. We can sympathize with Rahab but there is no virtue whatsoever in the lies of the others. The hallmark of Christianity is truth and this is not to be diluted in any way.

When God came to announce the coming of his Prince into this world there were no lies. Some parts of the announcement took some believing. For instance, how could a virgin have a baby? But there was no attempt to water down the message. The prophecies of the birth, life and death of the Prince of Peace were amazing in their detail. There are over 300 prophesies in the Old Testament literally fulfilled in Jesus. For instance his birth in Bethlehem is foretold in Micah 5:2, the entry into Jerusalem in Zechariah 9:9 and Psalm 22 and Isaiah 53 tell in detail of his death.

God had nothing to hide about his son and told it clearly and in remarkable detail.

Key Verse/Passage: Matthew 5: 33-37
Main Point: Simple honesty
Key themes: Keeping language simple & honest
The 'Story':   Was King Edward lying or being clever?
Application: Are lies ever right?

12

KING SOLOMON

Solomon was the son of David and followed his father to the throne of Israel in 970 BC. He was known for his remarkable wisdom, but it was not natural wisdom but a special gift of God to Solomon. God had said to Solomon 'Ask for whatever you want me to give to you', and he knowing the great difficulties of being king, asked that God would give him wisdom. God said, 'I will give you a wise and discerning heart'. This wisdom was put to a great test when two women came before the king both claiming to be the mother of the same baby. Solomon's judgment was that the baby should be cut in half and each woman have half each. One woman agreed but the other did not. The king said give the baby to the woman who did not agree to kill it for she is the mother.

The people were amazed at this decision and declared that Solomon 'had wisdom from God to administer justice'. But wisdom is a virtue that needs careful looking after and Solomon did not do this. By the end of his life he had turned away from God. He allowed his pagan wives to lead him into idol worship. This brought the anger of the Lord upon him and he lost his kingdom. It is incredible how such a wise man could finish up as he did, but it is a warning that we all need to keep close to God.

Wisdom is not an accumulation of knowledge. It is not the ability to pass exams. In the biblical sense it is the ability to judge correctly. For the Christian it is basically sanctified common sense. Do you have wisdom? How would you cope if faced with the two women Solomon had to deal with at the beginning of his reign? Can you see that we all need wisdom?

GOD'S WISDOM

Wisdom is far more than just an accumulation of knowledge· Wisdom is using knowledge for the highest and best ends. A man may have vast knowledge from many years of study and still lack wisdom in his use of that knowledge. Dr. Packer defines wisdom as 'the power to see, and the inclination to choose, the best and highest goal, together with the surest means of attaining it.'' This we find in God. He is, as Paul tells us, God only wise. Clearly God has all knowledge, but more than that, he is all-wise. What he knows he uses for good. In our God there is the awe-inspiring combination of wisdom and power. 'Wisdom and power are his' (Daniel 2:20).

'His wisdom is profound, his power is vast' (Job 9:4). This combination is important because it means that when God's wisdom seeks to do good it is never frustrated by lack of power to achieve its aim. Once again we see how all God's attributes hang together and feed and strengthen each other.

Wisdom is the ability to devise perfect ends and to achieve those ends by the most perfect means. Divine wisdom sees the end from the beginning, so there is no need to guess or calculate. Because of this all God's work is done in perfect wisdom and nothing he does could be done better.

God's wisdom should be a great encouragement to us and cause us to want to know something of it for ourselves. Do you remember Paul's thorn in the flesh in I Corinthians 12? What was the purpose of this? Why did God allow it? Paul knew: 'To keep me from becoming conceited because of these surpassingly great revelations, there was given me a thorn in my flesh.' Three times he asked God to remove it, but God would not. Instead Paul was told, 'My grace is sufficient for you, for my power is made perfect in weakness.' The reaction of the apostle to this was not to complain of God's action but to rejoice. Here was a man who saw the wisdom of God and knew that it would always work for his good.

Key Verse/Passage	1 Corinthians 1:24-25
Main Point	What is wisdom?
Key themes	How is Christ the wisdom of God?
The 'Story'	Solomon and the two women
Application	What would you have done in Solomon's place?

13

CONSTANTINE

In the fourth century persecutions and heresies plagued the church and did great damage, but perhaps the greatest damage was done by the so-called conversion of Constantine. This man was locked in battle with his rival Maxentius for the throne of the Roman Empire. The historian Eusebius tells us that before the crucial battle at the Milvian Bridge outside Rome on 27 October 312, Constantine saw in the sky a vision of a flaming cross with the words transcribed in Greek, 'By this sign conquer'. He put the sign of the cross on his soldiers' equipment and gained a great victory. He was convinced that the Christians' God had given him the victory and he now professed to being a Christian.

Whether Constantine was truly converted is open to serious doubt, but the Christian church was never the same again. It now had the official support of the Roman emperor, and while this certainly brought privileges (the greatest of these being the end of persecution), the price was enormous. Previously, to be a Christian involved great hardship; but now, to become a member of the church brought great social and political advantages. The result was that thousands joined the church who had had no experience of the new birth, and though the church grew much stronger in numerical terms, it was spiritually much weaker. Days of persecution were replaced by days of spiritual slackness and worldliness. The simplicity of earlier Christian worship gave way to the pomp and ceremony of pagan court practices. Constantine himself liked to dress in rich, ornate robes, and he presented a similar set of garments to the bishop of Jerusalem. Thus vestments were introduced for the first time, and other things like the use of candles and pilgrimages infiltrated Christianity from the pagan ceremonies of the court.

Worse still it now became a political advantage to be a church leader, and clergy fought each other for the right to be pastor of the Roman church.

The key to all this was Constantine's vision of the flaming cross. It certainly worked in that he won the battle, but how does this match up to the New Testament use of the cross? Does it not smack more of superstition than faith? There is a vast difference between superstition and faith. One relies on strange coincidences and the other on the word of God. One trusts in subjective feelings and the other in revealed truth. You can still see this today in the way the cross is worn as a lucky charm or the way footballers cross themselves before a match starts. These are far removed from the biblical teaching of the cross as a place of sacrifice for sin and atonement.

A man was painting the railings outside an evangelical church when a stranger came down the road. He asked if he could go into the church to pray.

'Of course', said the painter.

The man was only inside a few minutes when he came out saying, 'I can't pray in there, there are no crosses in there'.

How dark superstition can be. It binds the soul and deprives us of access to God.

How different this is from the faith exercised by King Asa in 2nd Chronicles 14. He had to fight an army much stronger than his but listen to his prayer as he led his men into battle, 'Then Asa called to the LORD his God and said, "LORD, there is no one like you to help the powerless against the mighty. Help us,

O LORD our God, for we rely on you, and in your name we have come against this vast army. O LORD, you are our God; do not let man prevail against you'".

Imitate this humble king who looked to the King of kings and Lord of lords as he faced insurmountable enemies. Resist the pull of superstition, and cast your burden on the Lord alone.

Key Verse/Passage	2 Chronicles 14: 11
Main Point	What is the difference between faith & superstition?
Key themes	Faith is in Christ not objects
The 'Story'	Asa from 2 Chronicles 14
Application	We can trust God

14

ALFRED THE GREAT

Alfred was the Saxon king of Wessex in the 9th century when the Danes were his great enemy. After he had lost one battle Alfred was fleeing for his life when he hid with a poor woodcutter and his wife. The few days he spent with them his mind was taken up with how to defeat the Danes. Nothing else mattered to the king.

The woman of the house was making cakes and she asked Alfred to keep an eye on them while she did something else. He agreed to do this but his mind was still taken up with the Danes and he forgot about the cakes and they burned. The woman was very angry and she told the king off severely, but of course she did not know he was the king. Alfred knew she was right and vowed never again to get so taken up with what he could or could not do to the neglect of what he should be doing.

How easy it is to have our minds full of great and important issues and neglect immediate matters that need attending to. The big issues are not to be forgotten but neither are the little matters to be ignored. Usually the little matters are the everyday things. For the Christian this means praying and reading the Bible. To neglect these will make us useless when called upon to face major spiritual battles.

The regular daily use of the Bible is crucial. If, as the apostle Peter says, the Bible is spiritual food for our soul and promotes spiritual growth, then daily feeding is obviously necessary. One of the major hindrances to spiritual growth is indwelling sin, and God's answer to this is Scripture–'I have hidden your word in my heart that I might not sin against you' (Psalm 119:11). Meditation implies thought, time and effort. It is quite the opposite to a casual dipping into Scripture. The person who is meditating is serious and not in a hurry. You will never benefit much from a reading of the Bible that is too quick and shallow.

No real Christian would deny the need for a daily use of Scripture, but very often the spirit is willing and the flesh is weak. How many times we make good resolutions to be more diligent in our Bible study, only to revert back to our old ways in a few weeks! So how do we combat this? Start by loving God's Word: if you do this you are halfway there. But you need also to recognize that there are two areas of Bible use—reading and studying.

This must be daily and systematic. Do not fall into the trap of reading in a haphazard way—dipping, in here and there to your favorite passages. The result of that will be that you know a few passages well, but the bulk of Scripture will remain a mystery to you. To overcome this, most of us need a system of Bible reading. There are many such systems available—some that enable you to read through the whole Bible in a year. But don't be too ambitious. Choose a system you can cope with, or one that you can adapt to suit yourself. If you don't, you can easily fall behind the quota of readings and get discouraged and give up. Set a pace that you can handle, and stick to it. It may be a chapter a day or ten chapters a day; only *you* know what your brain and workload can suitably benefit from. It is good also from time to time to read some of the shorter books of Scripture through in one sitting.

Ask your pastor or some older Christian what system of Bible reading they could recommend to you. System is crucial. If you fit in Bible reading when you can, then do not be surprised if you rarely fit it in at all. The devil will see to that.

What is the best time of day to read God's Word? There is no one answer to this, because it will vary with each one of us. Some people are useless in the morning, and others are useless late at night. A time when you can open the Bible with your mind alert and eager is the best time for you. The best time will differ also according to your responsibilities. A retired person with plenty of time is obviously different from a young mum with small children. Find out what suits you and stick to it. This involves self-discipline, but no one ever got anywhere in the Christian life without self-discipline.

Bible reading should always be linked to prayer. Each of these actually feeds and flows out of the other.

Key Verse/Passage	Psalm 1:1-2
Main Point	Get your priorities right
Key themes	How important is the Bible in your daily life?
The 'Story'	King Alfred and the Burning Cakes
Application	When nothing else matters to us, we sometimes forget what ought to matter most.

41

15

KING OFFA

In the eighth century Offa was king of Mercia. His kingdom stretched from the Thames Valley in the south to the Mersey River in the north. Its Western border was Shropshire. The dyke measured 20 meters across and averaged about four meters high. It was built to keep the Welsh out and to be a clear boundary of Offa's kingdom. It stretched 130 km from north to south.

Offa had very clear views of what belonged to him and the dyke reinforced this. No one could doubt what the dyke meant. It was said that if a Welshman was caught on the English side of the dyke he would have his ears cut off. And an Englishman caught on the Welsh side fared no better. Boundaries can be political niceties or severe demarcation lines. Offa's dyke was no nicety.

The Christian needs to have very clear demarcation lines in his life. He needs to know where the boundaries are and others need to know this to. The Bible tells us that 'we are in this world but not of it'. We are urged, 'Do not conform any longer to the pattern of this world, but be transformed by the renewing of your mind. Then you will be able to test and approve what God's will is—his good, pleasing and perfect will' (Rom. 12:2).

These are clear enough but they are not easy because the Christian is in a battle, and he is in a battle simply because he is a Christian. During 1941 London was bombed night after night by German planes. This bombing was known as the Blitz. Thousands were killed and whole areas of the city completely destroyed. It was a frightening time to live in England's capital city. Yet only 200 miles away in Paris no bombs were falling.

Why was London being blitzed and Paris not? The simple answer is that Hitler and his German army had already captured Paris. The French capital was no threat to him, hence no bombs. But London was a free city and very much opposed to Hitler. London was blitzed because it was at war with Hitler.

The Christian is at war with Satan and all the power of evil, so it is not surprising that Satan bombards us with all sorts of temptations and troubles. These are evidence of the war and proof that we no longer belong to Satan. We are free in the Lord Jesus Christ. Salvation has liberated us from the bondage of sin, and Satan does not like it. He cannot rob us of our salvation—that is secure in Christ—but he can make life uncomfortable for the believers. So when the battle gets hot, do not lose heart; just praise God that you are in the fight and not still in spiritual bondage.

So the Christian is at war with Satan and sin is always trying to invade our lives. How do we keep sin out? It's not easy but the psalmist points us in the right direction. 'I have hidden your word in my heart that I might not sin against you' (Psalm 119:11). The Bible is the most deadly weapon we have in our battle against sin.

The Bible is a unique book. There is nothing quite like this remarkable collection of 66 books written over a period of 1,500 years by 40 authors. It is crucial that we appreciate the uniqueness of Scripture. If the Bible is only a collection of old myths, then it would be stupid to accord it any authority. But the Bible claims to be much more. Its message is essential for salvation—'faith comes from hearing the message, and the message is heard through the word of God' (Romans 10:17). It is also essential for spiritual growth—'As newborn babes, desire the pure milk of the word, that you may grow thereby' (1 Peter 2:2 NKJV).

When we say that the Bible is the Word of God, we do not mean that God actually wrote it. He is its primary author, but it was written by human authors. But these were not expressing their own opinion— 'Above all, you must understand that no prophecy of Scripture came about by the prophet's own interpretation. For prophecy never had its origin in the will of man, but men spoke from God as they were carried along by the Holy Spirit' (2 Peter 1:20-21).

Key Verse/Passage	Romans 12:1,2
Main Point	Boundary lines in our lives
Key themes	Does Satan respect boundary lines?
The 'Story'	King Offa's dyke
Application	Keep your feet on the straight and narrow

16

BEWITCHED, BOTHERED & BEWILDERED

Many years ago there was a popular song entitled Bewitched, Bothered and Bewildered, and this title sums up how the Galatians had become by believing the false prophets.

The Galatians were certainly born again believers. There is no suggestion in the letter that they are anything but genuine Christians. This being the case Paul could possibly have said, 'they are saved and that is the main thing. It's a pity they have now believed lies but that does not change their salvation.' He could have said that, but he did not. On the contrary he was deeply grieved and concerned about them. Wrong doctrine has serious repercussions. Peter's actions in Galatians 2:11-14 led other Christians astray. But it also leads to wrong behavior and even more importantly it will rob God of glory.

So twice, in chapter 3 verse 1 and then verse 3, Paul calls the Galatians foolish. He is not referring to their intellect but to their lack of wisdom and sense.

The series of questions Paul asks them in verses 1-5 show how foolish they were. Paul had preached to them the cross and justification by faith, the Holy Spirit came upon them and they believed. There was no mention of anything other than Christ as the means of salvation. Jesus was their sufficiency and they gloried in the cross. Where was all that now?

Are you bewitched, bothered and bewildered? Are you becoming uncertain of biblical truths that you once firmly believed? Are you losing the joy you once had in the Lord

Jesus? If so, the problem you have is essentially the same as the Galatians. You have lost sight of the beauty and sufficiency of Christ. It is possible to understand someone becoming disillusioned with Christians, but how can any believer become disillusioned with Jesus? The Galatians had because they moved from adoration of Jesus to the rules and regulations of men. Have you done that? Or perhaps you have become fascinated not with man-made religion, but with the flashy attractions of the world. Or it may be that you have fallen in love with someone who is not a Christian and Christ is becoming a problem in that relationship.

It does not matter much what the bewitchment is, the result is always the same, and the answer is always the same. You need to get back to where you once were by fixing your heart and mind on Christ. It is foolish to be like Esau in the Old Testament and sell your birthright for a bowl of soup (Genesis 25:27-34).

There are Christians who are longing to know more of the Holy Spirit in their lives. That is good, but Paul reminds us all that every experience of the Holy Spirit is a result of faith and believing what we have heard of biblical truth. He roots this belief firmly in the fact of who Jesus is and what he has done for us. Therefore our business is to delight ourselves in Christ. We are to praise, adore, exalt and obey him in all things. If we depart from that, all sorts of problems will erupt. If we keep to it, the Holy Spirit will pour out divine favors so that we will have more and more of Jesus.

To prove this Paul turns us in Galatians 3 verses 6-9 to the life of Abraham. How did this great man get right with God? He was a man of faith. The righteousness that made him acceptable to God was not his own but one that had been credited to him, put to his account. It was faith in the love and grace of God that brought salvation to Abraham. In doing this the apostle makes a fascinating statement in verse 8, God "announced the gospel in advance to Abraham." The gospel was in the Old Testament. It is true that it was not there in its full New Testament glory, but the essence of it was there. In the Old Testament you will find that God saves sinners not on account of their goodness but on account of the righteousness he gives them.

Key Verse/Passage   Galatians 3:1
Main Point   Delight in Christ
Key themes   What is the joy of our salvation
The 'Story'   Paul & Peter's dispute....Gal 2: 11f
Application   Keep your eyes on Christ

17

RIGHT AND WRONG

There was a time when everyone knew what was right and wrong. Society had standards that were recognized, even if they were not always adhered to. Today all that has changed. Morality has died, and 'anything goes' has become the philosophy by which our nation lives or, perhaps more accurately, the philosophy by which it is dying. There is now no such thing as right and wrong, because there are no recognized absolute standards. So what was condemned thirty years ago, things like homosexuality, adultery, public nudity, foul language, are now acceptable. And to want to return to the old standards is regarded as total intolerance as puritanical.

Why has the change come about? Has there developed a more loving and gentle spirit in the land? No. The change is the result of a rejection of God and the Christian faith. It is not an expression of love, but an intolerance of anything that is biblical. For years we thought we could have the morality of the New Testament without the Christ of the New Testament. People would say that all we needed was the Sermon on the Mount and that Christian doctrine was divisive. Now even the Sermon on the Mount is regarded as too narrow and restrictive.

All this can be very confusing for a young believer. How can we live a Christian life in such a moral climate? We need to start by accepting that God's standards are absolute. For instance, what the Lord declared in the Ten Commandments thousands of years ago is still true today. It is still wrong to commit adultery or to covet. Moral standards are not to be dictated by the passing whims of society, but must be seen as the unchanging will of God. It may be that the world will never accept this, but the Christian must. Our standards must be those set out by God in the Bible, otherwise the Christian faith has no authoritative voice with which to speak to the world. A Christian faith which does not practice Christianity in life is nothing more than hypocrisy.

CONSCIENCE: A GIFT OF GOD

Conscience is the God-given ability to distinguish between right and wrong. Paul argues that this is as true of the unbeliever as it is of the believer (Romans 2:15). Men and women are not animals, and they have more than instinct with which to react to situations. They have a mind and will, and conscience uses these. Conscience is to the mind what pain is to the body. It warns that something is wrong and needs to be dealt with. But the conscience is not infallible and needs a standard to refer to.

By its abysmally low standard of right and wrong, and its refusal to accept guilt, society has effectively silenced the conscience. As a new Christian you are saved out of that kind of background and, in your new life, its influence has to be resisted and avoided.

A NEW STANDARD

The Christian's standard has to be the unchanging Word of God. Submission to the authority of Scripture in our everyday lives is the means by which sanctification (growth in holiness) is worked in us. The purpose of sanctification is to make us like Christ. This is God's desire for us and it ought to be the chief ambition of every believer. It is not easy, and if our standards are not the same as Christ's it will be totally impossible. So we need to learn to think biblically, to absorb the teaching of the Bible so thoroughly that it permeates our thinking and governs our desires. In this way our conscience will have the highest possible standard to which to relate.

When the Bible becomes our standard we will start to take God seriously, and only then will it be possible to take sin seriously. This will enable us to recognize our weaknesses and deal with them. We will be unable to tolerate what God hates. The greatest danger in the Christian life is to accept our sins as inevitable. If we believe we can do nothing about our sin, our doctrine of sanctification will be hopelessly wrong, because we are told very clearly in Romans 6 that we are dead to sin and we are not to let it reign in our bodies. Sin is no longer our master; therefore it cannot compel us to do anything. Sin can only operate in the Christian with his or her cooperation.

Withdrawing that co-operation is what the Bible calls putting sin to death. This is an obligation for all believers (Romans 8:12-13).

Key Verse/Passage	Romans 2:12-14
Main Point	Is morality dead?
Key themes	What determines what is right and wrong?
The 'Story'	John MacArthur's illustration
Application	Is sin inevitable? Explain.

18

THE ANCHOR HOLDS

There are times in our lives when circumstances make it necessary for us to be reminded of truths we know and love. Events happen that shake us and confuse us. We are bewildered as to what is happening. My third heart attack was like that with me. It was worse than the others and shook me, yes even frightened me. Now it is alright to be shaken or bewildered or frightened by events but it is not alright to allow those events to cause us to doubt God or to forget that the anchor holds even in the most adverse circumstance.

In Hebrews 6:19 we are told that we have an anchor for the soul, and this anchor is 'firm and secure'. Some Christians think that Heb. 6 teaches that the believer can lose his salvation. They look at verses 4-6 and say there it is, it's obvious. But it's not obvious. In fact Heb. 6 teaches the exact opposite—we can't lose our salvation. Why not? Because we have an anchor that holds us secure.

The key verse in the chapter is v. 9, 'we are confident of better things in your case things that accompany salvation.' What are the things that accompany salvation? What are the things that are true of the believer that give him eternal security?

The answer to these questions is the whole NT doctrine of salvation. We are always prone to minimize what God has done for us. Sometimes we talk of having 'accepted Jesus' or 'opened our heart to the Lord.', or 'made a decision'. When we turn to the Scriptures we find that salvation is far more wonderful than these phrases imply. The Bible teaches that it is God who has accepted us not we him (Eph. 1:6); it is God who opens hearts (Acts 16:14); it is God who chooses us (Eph. 1:4). In other words, from beginning to end God is the author of salvation.

Salvation is the glorious, thrilling work of God and that is why we can never lose it; that is why the anchor will always hold.

The believer is an heir of all this. He is an heir of salvation. How does one get to be an heir? One has to be chosen, favored. Very often the heir is one of the family but not always, A man leaves a will naming his heir and by definition the heir is someone with something coming to him. He does not have it yet but it is his, it's promised. He is chosen, his name is there. He may be unaware of it but he is the heir and the inheritance will come to him. All Christians are heirs of salvation. There was a time when they were not saved but even then they were heirs. They did not know it but they had been chosen by God the Author and Bestower of salvation. This gift was coming to them. They had been chosen, says the Bible, before the foundation of the world. This is thrilling. It is amazing. God's grace in salvation is so much bigger than we imagine.

We who are Christians are saved but in addition to that we have an anchor of the soul. The anchor is the gospel hope, it is Christ himself. Anchor is used for securing a ship, particularly in a storm. It is to prevent the ship drifting to its own destruction. The anchor is invisible, sinking beneath the waters it grips the rock. The winds may roar and batter the ship but the anchor keeps it safe. The ship may move a little but the anchor holds it secure. Unseen but sure the anchor never fails.

The storms of life may batter the believer, the devil hurls his fiery arrows at him, temptation seeks to move him away from his hope, but Christ his anchor holds him fast. And listen to this. v. 19 The anchor is fixed within the curtain, the veil, heaven itself. Christian your salvation is anchored in heaven. Nothing that happens in this world can therefore move it. "Firm and secure" says v. 19. Our security is entirely outside of ourselves. It is held fast by the risen, ascended, and glorified Lord Jesus Christ.

Key Verse/Passage	Hebrews 6:19
Main Application	Can we lose our salvation?
Key themes	Justification
The 'Story'	Peter's third heart attack
Application	Is Christ the Anchor enough to keep us safe?

19

YOU CLIMB AND I'LL PULL

Living the Christian life is a battle. It's hard. But then that is exactly what Jesus promised us. It is exactly what the Bible teaches from the Old to the New Testament. Jesus has saved us and nothing can change that. Heaven is guaranteed for all God's people but Jesus said that in this world you shall have trouble.

This is perfectly illustrated in the Old Testament when the Israelites under the leadership of Joshua were about to enter the Promised Land. The opening verses of Joshua emphasize that the Promised Land was God's gift to his people. They were not entitled to it. Neither they nor their ancestors had done anything to merit it. Neither would the blood and sacrifice of the ensuing battles warrant any idea that they had earned it. It was God's gift. Nevertheless they would not enter into possession of it without great effort. God required their obedience, and this meant that a very real responsibility was placed upon them. The land was God's gift, but they had to fight for every inch of it. This is a prime lesson from the book of Joshua that we must learn for the health of our own spiritual lives.

There is so much blessing for us in Christ, but it does not come easily. There are enemies who would seek to prevent us from enjoying all that God has for us. We have to fight, but we do so knowing that in Christ we are certain to win. However, verse 3 reminds us that the victory is one step at a time.

There may be some Christians who object that being victors in Christ sounds great, but it is not working for them. All they seem to experience is one defeat after another. One reason for this may be a lack of trust in God. There are many believers who want everything tied up neatly and tidily before they will do anything. Unlike Peter on the Sea of Galilee (Matt. 14:28-31), they would never even get out of the boat. It is easy to criticize Peter for becoming fearful, but at least he had the faith to trust Jesus and get out of the boat and walk on the water. Another reason is the failure to realize that God does not give us all the victory after one battle. We remember God's promise in Exodus 23:29-30: 'But I will not drive them out in a single year, because the land would become desolate and the wild animals too numerous for you. Little by little I will drive them out before you, until you have increased enough to take possession of the land.' We need to remember the words, 'little by little'.

Why did the Lord not deal with the Canaanites before Israel arrived? Why did they have to fight? Why does God not make it impossible for us to sin? Why do we have to face the continuous struggle against the world, the flesh and the devil? There are many answers to these questions and one is that 'little by little' keeps us in a state of constant dependence upon God. The battles are not so much to defeat the enemy, but to deal with our arrogance and self-confidence and to teach us more and more to lean upon the Lord.

We don't win the spiritual battles just by exercising will power. We need more than that. We need a sanctified life of obedience to the word of God.

Salvation is like being pulled out of a raging sea when waves were about to engulf you. You have been saved and the waves cannot harm you. You are safe—safe on the Rock, Christ Jesus.

But salvation is more than a rescue operation. You must go on to enjoy the life you were saved for. You are on the rock, and in front of you is a seemingly unclimbable steep cliff. You realize you could no more climb that yourself than you could have got out of the water yourself. Again, I stress, you are safe on the rock, but you want to go on and upward to the fuller life. The question is how? Then you see a rope hanging down from the top of the cliff, and you hear a voice shouting instructions to you and saying, 'You climb, and I will pull.'

That is sanctification. You are to climb over all the seemingly impossible obstacles that would try to keep you down, and at the same time God is drawing you upward and onward to Him.

Key Verse/Passage	Joshua 1:5
Main Application	You climb and I'll pull
Key themes	Why is the Christian life a battle?
The 'Story'	Joshua taking over from Moses
Application	Living sacrifice

20

BEWARE OF RATTLESNAKES

I've never been a good golfer but I always used to enjoy playing. I could hit a few good shots, but at the same time I was no stranger to the rough. The rough is the part of the course just off the fairway and, as the name implies, the ground here is rougher and the grass longer than on the fairway. So if you're in the rough, you're in trouble!

Playing back home in Wales I was used to the rough, and it was all part of the fun of the game. But one day playing in California I saw a sign in the rough which read 'BEWARE OF RATTLESNAKES'! This rough was no fun, it was dangerous. If ever there was an incentive to hit the ball straight and keep on the fairway, this was it. The incentive was great, but unfortunately it wasn't matched by my skill at golf and a few balls did fly off into the rough. I made no attempt to retrieve them, but left them to the rattlesnakes.

The Christian life is like a golf course. There are fairways, bunkers, and the dreaded rough. Our task as believers is to keep on the fairway because the rough has more deadly enemies than rattlesnakes for us. The devil, that old serpent, waits to ensnare the child of God.

When we become Christians we come into a living and personal relationship with God. We're now children of God and members of the household of faith. The implications of this for our lives are many and varied. But it doesn't mean that we never have any more problems or difficulties. Far from it. The experiences of God's people in Scripture show this. David spoke for us all when he wrote, 'A righteous man may have many troubles' (Psalm 34:19).

There are several reasons for this. No Christian is sinless, and often the repercussions of our sins cause us problems. Sometimes God has to teach us lessons that we will learn only in affliction, and therefore he allows trials to come into our lives. Then, of course, the devil is always seeking to make life difficult for God's people. So problems will come in all shapes and sizes. The important question is, 'How do we cope with them?'

Why is the Christian life such a battle? If God has done for us all that is described in the first three chapters of Ephesians, why do we struggle so much in the spiritual life, and why do we fail so often? The answer is given to us in Ephesians 6, verses 11, 12 and 16. We have an enemy, one who is at work with all his energies to pull us down. That enemy is the devil.

This battle is between God and Satan. Christ came into the world to get into the battle and to win it. The apostle John tells us that 'the whole world is under the control of the evil one', and that Jesus came into the world; 'to destroy the devil's work' (1 John 5:19; 3:8).

From Bethlehem to Calvary the battle raged. When Jesus was born, Satan used his puppet, King Herod, to try and kill the Savior. Satan failed, and Christ triumphed. At the beginning of Christ's public ministry Satan tried by a series of temptations to make the Savior sin. Once more the evil one failed. The greatest conflict was on Calvary's cross

The final and complete victory of Christ is in the resurrection, where Satan's greatest weapons, death and the grave, are swallowed up in Christ's victory.

All this does not mean, however, that the battle is over. The ultimate victory is assured, but the fight still goes on. Christ is not now in the world in person; but the church is. The church is His body, consisting of His people, and so Satan now carries on the conflict against Christians. That is why we are in the battle.

When you feel so poor that you begin to think you have no right even to pray, remember that your right does not depend upon your actions, but upon God's grace. Even when we are faithless, God always remains faithful. He is rich in mercy, even when we are poor in faith.

If you're in the rough in your Christian life and the rattlesnakes are threatening, get back on the fairway God has laid out for you. Remember Psalm 34:6, and cry to the Lord in the sure knowledge that he will hear and deliver you.

Key Verse/Passage	Psalm 34:19
Main Point	Get out of the rough
Key themes	Victory in Christ
The 'Story'	Peter's golf game in California
Application	More than conquerors

21

RUN YOUR CAR ON WATER?

Wouldn't it be great if you could run your car on water? Think of the advantages—for a start it would be cheaper. Today it costs a small fortune to fill the tank at the petrol station, but how much cheaper it would be to run a hose pipe from the kitchen tap. Also it would be safer. Water is not likely to catch fire like petrol. And water tastes nicer than petrol, so the advantages are great. There is only one disadvantage and that is that it would not work. Before this one disadvantage all the advantages become insignificant.

If you want your car to work properly do not put water in the petrol tank. Why not?—it is easier, cheaper, safer (it will not explode); it is more pleasant to taste and smell; and it is more convenient.

All that is true, but it will not work. Water in the petrol tank is alien to the efficiency of the engine. So too is worldliness in the Christian's life—it is easier, costs less and is perhaps more convenient; but it clogs up, slows down and grinds to a halt any spiritual progress.

Why is it today that so many Christians lack enthusiasm for the work of the gospel and lack commitment to the church? Why is the prayer meeting the most poorly attended meeting of the week? Why have we relegated evangelism to a special effort for week or so every couple of years instead of it being the ongoing work of the church every week? The answer to these questions is that we have been filling up our spiritual tank with water instead of the fire of the Holy Spirit.

FIRE

Our churches are, sometimes, very much like frozen food—cold, unattractive and unyielding, more at home in a fridge than anywhere else. But once let the heat get to it and everything changes.

The coldness disappears, the unattractive becomes appetizing, and the stiff and rigid becomes flexible and usable.

How we need the fire of God in our churches. By 'fire' we do not mean noise and nonsense but the warmth and passion of the Holy Spirit.

We need the fire of Mount Sinai, which brought before the people the sense of the holiness of God and the obedience he expected from them.

We need the fire of Mount Carmel, where God vindicated his own name through Elijah and false religion was blasted before the glory and power of the only true God. We need the fire of Pentecost, which resulted in thousands being saved.

Nearly five hundred times in Scripture, fire is used as a symbol of the presence of God. John the Baptist promised that Jesus would baptize his people with fire. The old Methodist, Samuel Chadwick, said, 'The supreme need of the church is fire. The baptism of the Spirit is the baptism of fire. Spirit-filled souls are ablaze for God. They love with a love that glows. They believe with a faith that kindles. They serve with a devotion that consumes. They hate sin with a fierceness that burns.' Who can deny our need today for this fire?

Pentecost was the fulfilling of the promise of Acts 1:8. Here was the power that Jesus said was crucial in order to evangelize the world. The physical phenomena, like wind and fire, are nothing like as significant as the spiritual power that came to all the believers. What happened did not affect only the apostles, but 'all of them were filled with the Holy Spirit'. With the Holy Spirit's power these men and women changed the world. The world misunderstood them (v. 13) but it could not ignore them (vv. 6-12).

Today we are facing a world that certainly does not understand Christianity but has no problem ignoring it. The world sees nothing in the church to attract it or disturb it, and it will have to be disturbed before it will be attracted to it. Before they ever heard the gospel the people at Jerusalem saw something in the first Christians that made them take notice.

Witnessing is more than telling people they need to be saved. Sinners need to see Christ in us. Is it not true that many people will not listen to the gospel because they have seen the shallowness and inconsistent lives of Christians? Therefore they will not go near a church. If our living does not attract people to Christ then our words never will. This brings us back to our supreme need to know the power of the Holy Spirit in our lives.

The Acts of the Apostles holds before us the enormous possibility, even in the most difficult times, when the power of the Spirit comes upon the church.

A.W. Tozer said, 'Where Jesus is glorified, the Holy Spirit comes. He does not have to be begged—the Holy Spirit comes when the Savior is glorified. When Christ is truly honored

Key Verse/Passage	Luke 3;16
Main Point	Substitutes are no good
Key themes	The Holy Spirit's power
The 'Story	Acts 2 and Pentecost
Application	The supreme need of the church

22

IT'S A BATTLE

'Come to Jesus, and all your problems will be over' is the message we hear from some preachers. Certain hymns, too, seem to confirm this teaching—like the chorus that ends, 'And now I am happy all the day.' Unfortunately, however, that is not the Christian's experience after conversion and, more importantly, that is not what the Scriptures teach.

When a person comes to Christ in repentance and faith, sin—his greatest problem—is dealt with. The joy of salvation and the experience of peace with God can be overwhelming, and with some this may last for days, weeks or even months. But eventually other problems, completely unknown in pre-conversion days, will begin to make themselves felt. As a result, far from being 'happy all the day', the young Christian will know the misery of doubts, guilt and conviction of sin as never before. On top of all this, he will have to face misunderstanding and opposition to his new-found faith from friends and relatives.

All this can seem quite devastating to the new convert, but the Scriptures assure us that it is only to be expected. The Lord Jesus Himself said to His disciples, 'In the world you will have trouble' (John 16:33). And the apostle Paul, returning to churches which he had established on his first missionary journey to strengthen and encourage them, told them, 'We must go through many hardships to enter the kingdom of God' (Acts 14:22).

Why should it be like this? The fact is that when we become Christians, we enter not a holiday camp where everything is jolly and comfortable, but rather a battle station in the middle of a fierce war. We are now soldiers in the Lord's army, and the enemy exerts tremendous pressure upon us. How we fare in this spiritual battle depends to a great extent upon how we are equipped.

The battle is very real. It is fierce, and at times devious and very confusing. The more we think of it, the more we wonder how we can possibly survive, let alone triumph. It is easy to sympathize with Jehoshaphat, king of Judah, who, on the approach of a huge enemy army, came before God and said, 'we have no power to face this vast army ... We do not know what to do' (2 Chronicles 20:12). But Jehoshaphat did not stop there; he went on to say, 'but our eyes are upon you'. His trust was in God, and the Lord rewarded that trust by telling him, 'the battle is not yours, but God's' (v.15). He was encouraged to stand firm and not lose hope because he was assured, 'the Lord will be with you' (v.17).

The battle is the Lord's, and we are only in it because we are His people. This does not mean that it is easy, or that all we have to do is stand aside and let God get on with it. God does not fight instead of us; we must fight, but in God's strength. The scriptural way is never, 'Let go and let God', but rather 'Pray much, and fight.' For every skirmish, for every trial, there is strength and power supplied to us by God, but we must use it. Of course, there are times when God intervenes directly; those are most thrilling experiences, but they do not invalidate the main principle which He Himself set down. The whole emphasis of this passage in Ephesians 6 is that it is God who supplies, but we who must use what He gives. How do we work this out in our lives?

FIGHT
Do not be afraid to get involved in the battle. The battle is unquestionably fierce and you will get battered and bruised. Scars may well be left, but we must not be afraid of this. Some Christians hear the noise of battle; they see the casualties and

they run. But that in itself is defeat. To let Satan march on unopposed is to deny our allegiance to Christ. Resist the devil, says James 4:7. Resist, not run. Whenever the enemy intrudes, confront him.

Notice that, in Ephesians 6: 12, Paul speaks of 'our struggle'— or, as the Authorized Version reads, 'we wrestle'. Wrestling involves personal contact—arms, legs and bodies entangled in confrontation. That is how the battle is. It is often a personal affair, with no-one else involved. Satan attacks you, and you resist. This is spiritual wrestling.

Key Verse/Passage	Acts 14;22
Main Point	The battle is the Lord's
Key themes	Resisting the devil
The 'Story'	The faith of Jehoshaphat in the face of danger
Application	Victory in Christ

23

NO LIMITS

In the New Testament (Romans 6:23) we are told that the wages of sin is death but the gift of God is eternal life.

The gift is the amazing and unbelievable response of the love of God to human sin. Who could have imagined it? Who could have thought that this was possible? We are entering a realm far beyond anything that the human mind can conceive.

Imagine it is your birthday and your family asks, "What do you want as a present?" You answer, "I'll have a new car, nothing fancy, just a Ford Focus, top of the range and automatic." They smile tolerantly and ask, "What color do you want your *cardigan* to be?" They love you, but there are limits to what gift they can give you.

GOD'S GIFT KNOWS NO SUCH LIMITATIONS AND ALL EXPECTATIONS ARE EXCEEDED

It's not your birthday now, but your death is very near. "What do you want?" asks God. You reply, "God, I don't want the wages. I don't want what I deserve. I want forgiveness for all my sin. I want acceptance by you. I want a guaranteed place in heaven."

"You shall have it," says God. "It is my gift to repentant sinners."

This is no exaggeration.

It is exactly what happens in salvation.

WHAT DOES THE BIBLE SAY ABOUT WAGES?
The Bible says there are three kinds of death: Spiritual, Physical, Eternal.

- Spiritual death is the separation of the soul from God.
- Physical death is the separation of the soul from the body.
- Eternal death is spiritual death made permanent.

WHAT DO MEN AND WOMEN SAY ABOUT DEATH
Here we see totally confused thinking, if there is any thinking at all. Man cannot understand that *when* the wage is paid is almost insignificant, but the fact that *it will* be paid is the all important matter.

Our view of death is both pagan and sentimental. A man in his 80's dies and we say, "It's to be expected, had a few good innings, it's a blessing." A person in his teens dies and we lament how tragic it is. Unfair, undeserved. We blame God and ask, "Why do the innocent suffer?" The Bible says the innocent do not suffer because there are no innocents. *All have sinned, there is none righteous, and death is the wage of sin.* Because men do not see death as spiritual and eternal, but only physical, they see it as the end, but it is not the end. The Bible says, "It is appointed unto man to die and *after* death the judgment."

This is why God's gift is so crucial.

The Australians are famous for the unique way they say, "Good day." Another expression with a meaning almost unique to the Australian is, "See you later." This is a warm, friendly way of saying goodbye. It may or may not have any relevance to actual reality, suggesting that a future meeting is planned. I remember a few years ago, after preaching in a church in Sydney, standing at the door afterwards to shake hands with the people. So many said to me, "See you later", that I began seriously to wonder if another meeting had been arranged for later that evening which no one had told me about. But there was no extra meeting; it was just their friendly way of saying goodnight.

God says to us all, "will see you later." He says this not only to Christians, but to atheists, humanists, and all sorts of unbelievers. The message of the gospel clearly reminds us that we are to see God later. And this is no friendly, harmless nicety, but the serious warning that we must all one day meet God.

When we see God, we will have to face the curse of the law, and, unless Jesus is your Savior, you do not have a hope.

Key Verse/Passage	Romans 6;23
Main Point	The guarantee of the gospel
Key themes	Meeting God
The 'Story'	The wages of death
Application	The gift of God

24

GUY FAWKES

Remember the fifth of November.
Gunpowder, treason and plot.
I see no reason why gunpowder, treason
Should ever be forgot...

The old rhyme was written so that we would not forget the origins of Guy Fawkes Day. In 1605 Guy Fawkes was part of a Catholic plot to blow up a Protestant parliament and impose Roman Catholicism on Britain. By today the origins have been long forgotten and November 5th is just an excuse for us to enjoy ourselves as we set off our fireworks and eat our hot dogs.

Origins are easily forgotten not only with Guy Fawkes Day but also with other things. Take for instance Christmas Day. The origin was God sending the Lord Jesus Christ into the world to save sinners. But today that is forgotten and December 25th just becomes an excuse for us to enjoy ourselves with drink and festivities.

Forgetting the origins of November 5th is not serious but forgetting what Christmas means is. If we forget the origins we forget that we are sinners who need a Savior; we forget that God hates sin and will not have it in his heaven; we forget that Jesus is the only answer to human sin. God never changes and neither does man. We are still sinners and Jesus is still the only Savior. History is full of plots by one religion against another but in all of history there is nothing like the story of Jesus. We dare not forget this.

The birth of Jesus was very special. The Old Testament prophet Isaiah, and the New Testament writers Matthew and Luke all tell us that his mother Mary was a virgin. His birth was not the result of human love or lust, but the remarkable life-giving operation of the Holy Spirit (Matthew 1:20; Luke 1:35). This may be baffling to our minds, but it is vital to our salvation. If Jesus was the result of a normal sexual relationship between a man and woman, he would be like all men—a sinner by nature and helpless to save himself, let alone anyone else. Jesus did not inherit a sinful nature, and his life of obedience to the law of God kept his nature sinless and pure. In his life he was 'tempted in every way, just as we are—yet was without sin' (Hebrews 4:15).

This is of more than passing interest. It is crucial for our salvation. Jesus came to make atonement for our sin. That meant he had to die in our place, for that was the penalty God had decreed for sin. He came therefore to die as a sacrifice for us—to die in our stead. That was God's plan: 'He was pierced for our transgressions, he was crushed for our iniquities; the punishment that brought us peace was upon him, and by his wounds we are healed' (Isaiah 53:5).

Beware of Rattlesnakes

Charles Spurgeon says of Guy Fawkes Day, 'This day ought to be celebrated, not by the saturnalia of striplings, but by the songs of saints. Our Puritan forefathers most devoutly made it a special time of thanksgiving. There is extant a record of the annual sermons preached by Matthew Henry on this day. Our Protestant feeling, and our love of liberty, should make us regard its anniversary with holy gratitude. Let our hearts and lips exclaim, "We have heard with our ears, and our fathers have told us the wondrous things which thou didst in their day, and in the old time before them." Thou hast made this nation the home of the gospel; and when the foe has risen against her, thou hast shielded her. Help us to offer repeated songs for repeated deliverances. Grant us more and more a hatred of Antichrist, and hasten on the day of her entire extinction. Till then and ever, we believe the promise, "No weapon that is formed against thee shall prosper." Should it not be laid upon the heart of every lover of the gospel of Jesus on this day to plead for the overturning of false doctrines and the extension of divine truth? Would it not be well to search our own hearts, and turn out any of the Popish lumber of self-righteousness which may lie concealed therein?'

Key Verse/Passage	Psalm 77
Main Point	Remember what God has done
Key themes	How can we remember?
The 'Story'	
Application	Spurgeon on Guy Fawkes day

25

NO WAITING LISTS WITH GOD

The heart surgeon told me that I had a serious heart condition and needed a bypass operation. I asked him when this would be done. He replied that he was putting me on his waiting list. He said that I was 98th on his list and he was doing two operations a week. So I was not likely to get the operation for at least a year. I said if I had a serious heart condition I could be dead by then. He agreed but said that that was how it was.

Some time before this God told me through his Word and the preaching of the gospel that spiritually I had a serious heart condition. It was urgent and terminal and needed seeing to at once. Fortunately there was no waiting list with God. What needed to be done could be done at once.

To do my bypass the hospital surgeon had to cut open my chest to get at the heart. God also has to cut. In the words of Acts 2:37 it is a cutting to the heart. In other words God causes us to be deeply aware of our sin and our need of salvation. There is no waiting list with God because on the cross Jesus did all that was necessary to deal with human sin. He took the guilt and punishment that sin deserved and died in the sinners place. God is now able to take away the heart of stone, that sin has left in every one of us, and replace it with a heart of flesh. (Ezekiel 36:26).

Our problem is that we have an 'unbelieving *heart* that turns away from the living God'. We see the consequence of this in Genesis 6, 'And God saw that the wickedness of man was great in the earth, and that every imagination of the thoughts of his heart was only evil continually'. If you don't believe that then just look at your own heart and ask if this is not true of you.

The gospel reduces us all to a mass of quivering jelly. It cuts to the heart. It does not puff up but pulls us down. We feel we are totally unqualified for heaven and completely hopeless before God.

But that is not true. Do you want to be a Christian? Then you are qualified because all the qualification God requires is that you be a sinner. In that no one is more qualified than you.

You say you have no hope of being acceptable to God—that's true if you are relying on yourself. But the gospel offers us another hope—Jesus. This is amazing! You are offered the qualification of Jesus—his holiness, his goodness, sinlessness, character. That is an infallible hope.

Cut to the heart? If you have been you will be asking, what shall we do? Repent—see how hopeless you are if left to yourself but see also the glorious hope you have in Jesus.

Cut to the heart? A person is never so near to grace as when he feels hopeless and guilty.

The hospitals have waiting lists because their resources are finite. The National Health Service, good though it is, cannot meet the demands made upon it.

God has no such problems. He saves everyone who comes to him in repentance and faith. No one is turned away disappointed and disillusioned. The heart job God does is guaranteed to last a lifetime and never need repeating. God promises, 'I will give them an undivided heart and put a new spirit in them.'

I am thankful for the heart bypass operation I had twenty years ago. Without it I would be dead by now, but I know it will not last forever. The work of grace God did in me will last forever. If you want God to deal with the sin of your heart then come to him and ask him to do it for you. There are no waiting lists so come now.

Key Verse/Passage	Ezekiel 36;26
Main Point	What is a heart of stone?
Key themes	What is the qualification of Jesus?
The 'Story'	The Lost Son Luke 15
Application	Now is the day of salvation

26

WRITTEN OFF

My wife had an accident in our car the result of which was that the car was written off. It was not a bad accident and thankfully no one was hurt, but the insurance company decided that our eight year old Ford was a write off. It was not worth the cost of the repairs to put it right. It was scrapped.

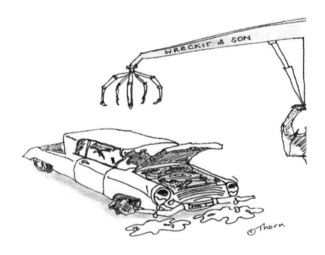

As God looks at mankind ruined by the ravages of sin he says, it's a write off. There is no possibility of repair. That is why the New Testament language describing men and women in sin is extreme. Sinners are not sick needing healing; they are not scarred needing patching up; they are dead, needing new life.

The problem is not moral or social, it is spiritual. It is to do with the relationship between the holy God and his sinful creations.

Man is not as God made him. He was made in the image of God but sin has shattered that image. At the beginning of time man was the final and greatest act of creation, because man was made in the image of God. This was not a physical image but it means that man is distinct from every other creature in that he has a capacity for fellowship with and enjoyment of God. There was a sweet and blessed oneness between God and man. Everything needed for life and happiness God gave man.

That is how God made man. Sinless and perfect. But things changed!

MAN AS SIN MADE HIM
There are people today foolish enough to think that sin makes no difference. It is played with, applauded, made the centre of entertainment and generally looked upon as harmless. Then we wonder why the world is in the mess it is in with so much war, crime and turmoil. The world is as it is because man is not as God made him, but as sin has made him.

What has sin done to men and women? Man was made sinless but when sin entered his nature (we read of this in Genesis 3) everything changed. Man led by Satan rebelled against God and this ruined man's relationship with God. The result was that man becomes alien to God and sin reigns in his life. And because of sin death now becomes a terrible part of man's experience. The image of God was shattered. Of course sin makes a difference. Men and women are now enemies of God and come under divine wrath and judgment.

MAN AS CHRIST CAN RE-MAKE HIM
In spite of our sin God still loves us and seeks to re-make us and destroy the influence of sin in our lives. The gospel tells us how God does this. In Ephesians 2:10 we are told that the Christian is God's workmanship, and in John 3:3 Jesus uses the phrase 'born again' to describe how this work of re-making begins.

God sent Jesus into this world to deal with human sin and to save sinners. This he does by becoming the sinner's substitute. He takes the responsibility for our sin and with this goes the guilt and punishment. The sinless Jesus faces the wrath of God instead of us. This is what the cross is about. On the cross death, the punishment for sin, falls on Jesus instead of upon us. The substitute bears the penalty we deserved.

The prophet Isaiah says of Jesus, "He was pierced for our transgressions, he was crushed for our iniquities;...by his wounds we are healed. We all, like sheep have gone astray, each one of us has turned to his own way; and the Lord has laid on him the iniquities of us all." Isaiah 53:5-6

The whole thing is incredible but true. This is the gospel and it is an amazing message.

Now as a result of what Jesus has done God is able to forgive us for our sin, but more than that he makes us new creatures with a new nature and a renewed relationship to himself. The saved sinner is accepted as a child of God. He is born again. He has new life in Christ.

All this is offered us in the gospel. To the guilty sinners comes the offer of a full pardon for all sin and adoption into God's family. Without this we are in a hopeless and lost position.

"And this is the testimony; God has given us eternal life, and this life is in his Son. He who has the Son has life; he who does not have the Son of God does not have life." (1 John 5:11)

Key Verse/Passage	1 John 5:11
Main Point	Man as Christ can remake him
Key themes	Jesus our Substitute
The 'Story'	Isaiah 53
Application	No one is too bad to be saved

27

BIG WORDS

If you consider big words, there are very few bigger than the name of that town in North Wales, which is called – Llanfairpwllgwyngyllgogerychwyrndrobwyllllantysiliogogogoch. The name translates as *"St Mary's Church in the hollow of the white hazel near a rapid whirlpool and the Church of St Tysilio of the red cave"*.

A local committee was formed to try and encourage trains, travelers and 19th Century tourists to stop at the village in order to help develop the village as a commercial and tourist centre. It is believed the name was conceived by a cobbler, or a tailor, depending upon what story you hear, from Menai Bridge. Little did they know at the time that they had invented one of the most successful tourist promotional plans of all time. Today the village is signposted as Llanfairpwllgwyngyll and is known by locals as Llanfairpwll or Llanfair. It is also known as Llanfair PG to differentiate it from other Welsh "Llanfair" villages. So many names for just the one place! Such a large name for such a tiny place!

The Christian faith also has its share of big words. Perhaps the least understood is PROPITIATION. We find this in the Authorised Version translation of Romans 3:25, 'Whom God hath set forth to be a propitiation through faith in his blood, to declare his righteousness for the remission of sins that are past, through the forbearance of God;' Many modern translations do not use the word. They prefer easier understandable words, and that is ok as far as it goes so long as they not also change the meaning as well as the word. Changing the long Welsh name for LlanfairPG is no problem because they can always pull out the full name at the railway station for the tourists and no harm is done. But to change the meaning of propitiation is fatal because it is the heart of the Christian faith.

The propitiation means that on the cross, bearing our sin and guilt, Jesus faced the wrath of God instead of us, and fully paid on our behalf the debt we owed to the broken law of God. At Calvary Jesus made it possible for a holy God to be propitious— or favorably inclined—towards us, even though we are guilty sinners. God dealt with the problem of sin in the only way that could satisfy his holy justice and enable him to save a people who deserved only judgment.

Another long word that is often used in conjunction with propitiation is the word SUBSTITUTION or SUBSTI- TUTIONARY DEATH OF JESUS. This again is a word that we cannot play around with if we are to keep to New Testament teaching.

Consider carefully the following statements:
The Lord has laid on him the iniquity of us all (Isaiah 53:6).
He himself bore our sins in his body on the tree (1 Peter 2:24).
God made him who had no sin to be sin for us (2 Corinthians 5:21).

Each of these passages tell us that Jesus died *in our place*. We deserve to die, but he died instead of us. He became our substitute. To use an Old Testament illustration, he became the 'scapegoat' (Leviticus 16)—the innocent victim bearing the guilt of others and suffering their just punishment. This was God's plan to make salvation possible for guilty sinners.

The big words of Christianity are not big because of the words in them, but because of the gospel truths in them. Their content is huge and their significance is gigantic. This is what makes them big.

Key Verse/Passage	Romans 3:25
Main Point	Jesus dying for me
Key themes	The scapegoat
The 'Story'	The Cross
Application	There is nothing bigger than the gospel

28

WHAT IF CHRISTMAS WAS IN JUNE?

If Christmas was in June we could stop dreaming of a white Christmas and Rudolph the red nosed reindeer would not have been invented. Many of our Christmas traditions are the result of the holiday being held in mid-winter. But Christmas is not in mid-winter everywhere. Several years ago I was in Australia for Christmas and there December is in the middle of summer. So I was looking forward to a hot, sunny Christmas, but it rained all day.

Christmas could be held in June because we do not know exactly when Jesus was born, but it should make no difference to the meaning of Christmas. Christmas is about the birth of Jesus Christ and God's gift to sinful men and women of a Savior. It is about the greatest miracle of all when God became man. The theological word which describes this is incarnation, which means 'in the flesh'. Listen how the apostle John describes this in John 1:14 'The Word became flesh and lived for a while among us.' John had already told us that the Word was God. God became man in the person of Jesus Christ. God identified himself with man in a way he had never done before.

God had always been with his people. He was with Moses when he led the people in the Exodus. He was with David when he fought Goliath. If he was not with them they could never have been successful. But in Jesus he is with us not merely by helping us but in that he took human nature so that Jesus was the God/Man, fully God and fully man. The reason for this is told us in Hebrews 2:17-18, 'For this reason he had to be made like them, fully human in every way, in order that he might become a merciful and faithful high priest in service to God, and that he might make atonement for the sins of the people. Because he himself suffered when he was tempted, he is able to help those who are being tempted.'

Jesus had to become a man in order to make atonement for man's sins. It was man who had broken God's law and sinned, therefore it had to be man who would pay the penalty for that sin. But there was no man qualified to do this, so God became man in the person of Jesus Christ and did for us what was crucial to our salvation.

Jesus was more than a man. Twenty-five times in the Gospels he calls himself the Son of God. Jesus is Emmanuel, which means 'God with us'. It is true that God had always been with his people and we can see in the Old Testament that he was with Moses and David. However, in Jesus, God was with us in a very different way. In Jesus, God becomes man, takes to himself human nature and identifies himself with us in a way the Old Testament saints never experienced.

Jesus is truly man and truly God. He is not part man and part God. In him exists two natures so that he is divine and also sinless man. The sinners only hope rests on this great truth of who Jesus is, because God can only be known through the Lord Jesus Christ.

The key factor in understanding the birth of Jesus is God's attitude to human sin. God is angry at sin and God's wrath is his anger against those who sin and his determination to punish them. That is not a very popular belief these days, but unquestionably it is what Jesus taught. God, who is completely holy, cannot regard evil and good in the same way. He cannot smile benevolently upon both truth and lies. So God's holiness makes hell as inevitable as his love makes heaven.

God never excuses sin, but in his love and mercy he is willing to pardon and forgive the sinner, but only on his terms. The terms are that the sin must be dealt with and punished, and the sinner must turn to him in repentance and faith.

Jesus had to become a man in order to deal legally and justly with our sin. It was man who had broken God's law and sinned, therefore it had to be man who would pay the penalty for that sin. But there was no man qualified to do this, so God became man in the person of Jesus Christ and did for us what was crucial for our salvation.

Key Verse/Passage	John 1:14
Main Point	Who is Jesus?
Key themes	Why did Jesus become Man?
The 'Story'	
Application	Only one way to God

29

WHITSUN

The Bible has but one basic message—the glory of God in our salvation. And the three great events in the ministry of Jesus all proclaim the same message. Each is about salvation and each shows clearly that salvation is completely dependent upon God.

1. Christmas—if God did not become man, salvation would be impossible.
2. Easter—if Jesus did not die for us, our sins could not be forgiven, and his resurrection assured his victory.
3. Whitsun—if the Holy Spirit had not been poured out, we would never see our need of salvation and turn to Christ.

Whitsun shows us the way God applies the gospel to men and women dead in sin. Here we have all the essential ingredients of salvation—preaching the gospel; the power of the Holy Spirit; men and women convicted of sin, and repentance.

And at Whitsun, the Holy Spirit, using the preaching of the cross, saved 3,000 souls. That is God's way. It always has been and still is today.

For seven weeks the church had the facts of the cross and the resurrection, but they saw no conversions. Facts alone, however glorious and however well presented have no converting power. Whitsun set the facts on fire by setting the church on fire. The first result of the fire was that unbelievers heard the wonders of God (v.10); this led to 3000 being saved (v. 41).

Are you saved? What happened on the first Whitsun is still happening today, but has it happened to you?

Our sin brings us under the judgement of God and being saved means we are saved from the consequence of that sin, which is death and hell.

Pentecost or Whitsun was the fulfilling of the promise of verse 8 in chapter 1. Here was the power that Jesus said was crucial in order to evangelize the world. The physical phenomena, like wind and fire, are nothing like as significant as the spiritual power that came to all the believers. What happened did not affect only the apostles, but 'all of them were filled with the Holy Spirit'.

With the Holy Spirit's power these men and women changed the world. The world misunderstood them (v. 13) but it could not ignore them (vv. 6-12).

Today we are facing a world that certainly does not understand Christianity but has no problem ignoring it. The world sees nothing in the church to attract it or disturb it, and it will have to be disturbed before it will be attracted to it. Before they ever heard the gospel the people at Jerusalem saw something in the first Christians that made them take notice.

Witnessing is more than telling people they need to be saved. Sinners need to see Christ in us. Is it not true that many people will not listen to the gospel because they have seen the shallowness and inconsistent lives of Christians? Therefore they will not go near a church. If our living does not attract people to Christ then our words never will. This brings us back to our supreme need to know the power of the Holy Spirit in our lives. *The Acts of the Apostles holds before us the enormous possibility, even in the most difficult times, when the power of the Spirit comes upon the church.* Tozer said, 'Where Jesus is glorified, the Holy Spirit comes. He does not have to be begged —the Holy Spirit comes when the Savior i⁻ glorified. When Christ is truly honored.'

The most important thing about Pentecost was not speaking in tongues but the fact that 3,000 souls were saved (v. 41). The tongues are not unimportant but Pentecost is about the Holy Spirit's work of salvation. This is proved by the fact that tongues are rarely mentioned in the rest of Acts, but almost every page is taken up with salvation. Peter quotes the Old Testament prophet Joel (v. 21) to explain what has happened in terms of souls being saved. He then goes on immediately to speak of the death and resurrection of Jesus. This is because it is in Jesus alone that God deals with our sin and provides pardon and forgiveness for the guilty sinner.

The whole sermon is fixed firmly in the Old Testament Scriptures. It centers on who Jesus is and what he has done, and concludes with a call for repentance. 3,000 people responded to that message and were saved.

The Bible has but one basic message—the glory of God in the salvation of sinners.

Key Verse/Passage	Acts 2:41
Main Point	God's way of salvation
Key themes	Salvation is crucial
The 'Story'	Acts 2—Pentecost
Application	Are you saved?

30

TRUTH OR TRADITION?

Truth and tradition have always been in contention. And this is especially true when it comes to the subject of Christmas. This is a season full of traditions from Santa Claus to Rudolph the reindeer to Christmas trees. These are harmless and happy traditions except when they push the truth out of Christmas.

The truth is that Christmas is the invention of God. By Christmas I don't mean December 25th but the birth of the Lord Jesus Christ, the Son of God, and the Savior of the world. The truth is that God planned this event in all its details. He prophesied it in the Old Testament and then brought it about at exactly the time He wanted. Galatians 4:4 'But when the set time had fully come, God sent his Son, born of a woman, born under the law, to redeem those under the law, that we might receive the full rights of sons.'

John Stott says of this verse, 'Notice that God's purpose was both to 'redeem' and to 'adopt'; not just to rescue from slavery, but to make slaves into sons. We are not told here how the redemption was achieved, but we know from Galatians 1:4 that it was by the death of Christ and from 3:13 that this death was a 'curse-bearing' death. What is emphasized in these verses is that the one whom God sent to accomplish our redemption was perfectly qualified to do so. He was God's Son. He was also born of a human mother, so that He was human as well as divine, the one and only God-man. And He was born 'under the law', that is, of a Jewish mother, into the Jewish nation, subject to the Jewish law. Throughout His life He submitted to all the requirements of the law. He succeeded where all others before and since have failed: He perfectly fulfilled the righteousness of the law. So the divinity of Christ, the humanity of Christ and the righteousness of Christ uniquely qualified Him to be man's redeemer. If He had not been man, He could not have redeemed men. If He had not been a righteous man, He could not have redeemed unrighteous men. And if He had not been God's Son, He could not have redeemed men for God or made them the sons of God.'

That is not tradition. That is truth. The traditions of men are pathetic compared with the wonder and glory of these truths. Is there anything more amazing than God becoming man in order to save sinners? People today have difficulty believing in miracles. While books like Harry Potter always top the sales charts, the Bible's emphasis upon the supernatural is dismissed as impossible. The miraculous and supernatural are alright in stories, but we can't be expected to take them seriously. We think that if we can't do miracles, then neither can God. We impose our human limitations upon God. But God isn't like us, and nowhere is this seen more clearly than in the Christmas story.

The miracle of Christmas is that God became man. This is the greatest miracle of all, and if we can believe this, then every other miracle becomes inevitable.

THE WORLD NEEDS A MIRACLE
The first century world into which Jesus was born was no different, morally and spiritually, from our twenty first century. It was in a mess. Who can deny the mess of our day? Terrorism, rampant crime, greed in business, broken families ... the list is endless. Every copy of a newspaper and every TV news program emphasizes the mess we're in.

Why is this? It's not because of economic, social or politic reasons—the problem is spiritual. Rich and poor, we're all in the same spiritual and moral mess, and no one has an answer.

No one, that is, except God. God has the answer.

The answer is not tradition but to get back to the truth about Christ. This isn't a fairy story. It is very, very real. The Apostle Peter addressed this head on when he said in his last letter before martyrdom, "We did not follow cleverly invented stories when we told you about the power and coming of our Lord Jesus Christ, but were eyewitnesses of his majesty" (2 Peter 1:16). There is, even for us today, the possibility of salvation. Salvation means being saved from the consequences of our sin. It means being acceptable to God, and only Jesus can make this possible for us.

Jesus is the only Savior because He is the only Savior God has provided. He alone is both God and man, and so ... He is the only one who could possibly achieve salvation for us. What God offered that first Christmas 2000 years ago, He still offers today—the day of salvation is not yet over

Key Verse/Passage	Galatians 4:4
Main Point	The miracle of Christmas
Key themes	The mess the world is in
The 'Story'	The birth of the Lord at the perfect time
Application	Jesus is the only Savior

31

HOT CROSS BUNS

Nearly everyone likes a hot cross bun. These delicious cakes were intended to be eaten at Easter but they are so good that it's possible to get them all the year around. They were intended to focus people's minds upon the cross and all it means. It's a pity this good intention has long ago ceased but we still need to ask the question, 'what is the cross of Jesus all about?'

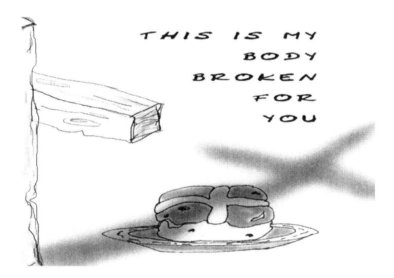

The message of the cross speaks of human sin and guilt, and of divine wrath and judgment. Today, people reject both sin and judgment, so they change the message of the cross. They sentimentalize it or shroud it in superstition so that the cross becomes nothing more than a lucky charm. Basically, men reject the cross as God's answer to human sin because they do not see sin as a problem. Therefore, there's no need for an answer. But the fact is that men and women are perishing and going to hell.

God warns us over and over again in the Bible of the terrible consequence of sin. The message of the cross comes to us with its invitation of salvation, but also with its warning if we reject the message—and yet still men reject it; they do not take their sin seriously.

The death of Jesus, both with regard to its manner and its purpose, was set and determined by God Himself. It wasn't a last minute adjustment to a plan that was going wrong. It always was the plan, as the many references and allusions to the cross in the Old Testament make clear. To the Christian, this is a thrilling truth because it puts our salvation at the heart of God's will and purpose for this world. When Jesus died it was an act of substitution and propitiation—he died instead of me, and in his death he paid the price for my sin.

That God is 'love' is a precious truth that is accepted by practically everyone, but the meaning we give to love is not always biblical. Modern man confuses love with sentimentality, and sees God's love as a sort of general benevolence which has no other purpose but our happiness. It then follows that God will not punish sin. Consequently, every notion of hell is dismissed as incompatible with the idea of a God of love.

Such thinking is seriously flawed because, although it's true that 'God is love', this is not the only thing that's true about God. He is also holy. The love of God as seen on the cross saves sinners, but what are they saved from? The Bible has only one answer to that. Men are saved from the consequence of their sin, from the wrath and judgment of God upon that sin. Why in John 3:16 are people perishing? Because God is holy and will not, and cannot, tolerate sin. In 1 John 4:9-10, we see both the love and holiness of God linked together: 'This is how God showed His love among us; He sent His one and only Son into the world that we might live through Him. This is love; not that we loved God, but that he loved us and sent His Son as an atoning sacrifice for our sins.' Why was it necessary for Jesus to be an atoning sacrifice or propitiation for our sins? Because God in His holiness had declared that the wages of sin was death. He will not wink at human sin or pretend it's nothing. It has to be dealt with in accordance to His own law. That's what the cross is about.

The cross is the place where God deals once and for all with our sin. It is from the cross that Jesus prays, 'Father, forgive them' (Luke 23:34). How do men react to this great demonstration of love and mercy? Man's reaction down through the centuries is clearly mirrored in the reaction of the two criminals on either side of the Savior and the crowd looking on.

Those in this passage who rejected salvation have a common bond; it is the 'if' of doubt. Notice that the rulers (v. 35), the soldiers (vv. 36,37), and the criminal (v. 39), all expressed doubt at the claims of Jesus to be the Savior. One man at least, at Calvary, saw and believed.

Saved (v. 43). In the morning the man was a condemned criminal; by the afternoon he was a redeemed sinner; by the evening he was a glorified saint. Such is the greatness of the love and mercy of God. Well does the hymn-writer say:

'The dying thief rejoiced to see that fountain in his day
And there may I as foul as he wash all my sins away.'',

Key Verse/Passage	1 John 4:9-10
Main Point	The message of the cross
Key themes	The love of God and the holiness of God
The 'Story'	The transformation of the converted thief
Application	The necessity of the cross

32

DE-ICING

In March 1994, I was due to fly out of JFK Airport in New York at 6:15 p.m. The flight was delayed for three and one-half hours and the reason was ice. In the afternoon there had been a light snowfall—only about two inches. When it came down it looked lovely. The houses and trees were covered with a beautiful coat of white, but at the airport it caused havoc.

The snow settled on the planes and froze. This made a safe take-off impossible so every plane had to be de-iced. Large trucks came along side our plane and with high pressure jets sprayed the whole of the fuselage with hundreds of gallons of de-icing fluid. It only took twelve minutes to do the job, but it was absolutely crucial. The ice on the wings did not look like much of a problem, but it was enough to prevent the airliner from doing what it was made to do and going where it was intended to go. That marvellous piece of engineering was earthbound, crippled by the cold grip of ice. But soon the ice melted under the power and pressure of the de-icing jets, and in a short time we were airborne.

SPIRITUALLY EARTHBOUND
As I sat in the plane and watched the de-icing process I thought of the many times that my Christian life had been earthbound and prevented from doing what God had saved me to do. So often as Christians we let the icy grip of materialism and worldliness, or fear and depression hold back any real progress

in our spiritual lives. Coldness towards God stifles prayer, and we know so little of soaring on eagle's wings.

We allow many things to come into our lives that, like the falling snow, look so attractive and harmless, but when they settle, they mold to our lives like the ice on the fuselage of the plane. The result is the same. We need a spiritual de-icing. We need to feel again the cleansing and purifying jets of God's love and grace melting us and fitting us to soar into the heavenly realms of fellowship with the Lord. We need to be doing what God saved us to do and going where he wants us to go.

The de-icing of the plane did not take long and neither does it take long for a believer to be brought back into a right relationship with God.

Christian, do you believe that?

It may be that you can see yourself sitting on the runway like that frozen plane. You have been there for years and see very little hope of change. Perhaps you are afraid to try and take off because of fear of a crash.

God can restore in a moment all the wasted years of cold, empty religion. The fire of the Holy Spirit is the only effective remedy to the ice of cold, formal, lifeless Christianity.

Are you earth-bound? Have you forgotten what it is like to soar on wings like eagles? Then seek the Lord for forgiveness and renewal. Look to Him. Draw near to God, and He will draw near to you.

THE REMEDY
As I watched the de-icing of the plane I thought of the cold winter mornings at home when I have to de-ice the windshield of the car with a little aerosol can. I thought how useless it would be trying to de-ice a huge airliner with a can of aerosol.

But don't we try small remedies to our spiritual problems when what we need is a drenching in the love and grace of God?

The Bible talks of grace abounding and love lavished upon us, so there is no shortage of the remedy. The question is, do we want it? As God made the eagle to soar in the sky, so we Christians are made not to be spiritually earthbound but to enjoy all that the Lord has for us.

If we took the Scriptures seriously then two little words would transform our Christian lives, transform our churches and transform our society—*DO IT.*

A man dead in sin can do nothing to change his spiritual condition. But a saved man is no longer spiritually dead. He has been born again, he is alive in Christ, and therefore spiritual activity is possible.
- He can be more prayerful,
- more obedient,
- more submissive to God.
  So DO IT.

- He can be less critical,
- less jealous,
- and less envious.
  So DO IT.

Key Verse/Passage Isaiah 40:29-31
Main Point   What is a spiritual de-icing
Key themes   Wanting the remedy
The 'Story'   The grounded plane
Application   Are you spiritually earthbound

33

BY FAITH

'By faith Moses when he had grown up, refused to be known as the son of Pharaoh's daughter. He chose to be ill-treated along with the people of God, rather than to enjoy the pleasures of sin for a short time. He regarded disgrace for the sake of Christ as of greater value than the treasurers of Egypt because he was looking ahead to his reward.' (Hebrews 11:24-26). By faith Moses did something.

There are many definitions of faith and you've got a great one at the beginning of this chapter. But basically if you want a simple definition of faith, *faith means to believe and to trust God.* That's basically it in its very fundamentals. It's to believe and to trust God. That's why faith comes by hearing the word of God. If there is no word of God to hear, then there can be no faith. Now that's true because of what faith is, faith is not, it is most definitely not, a step in the dark. That's what you hear faith defined as sometimes, as a step into the dark. It isn't that, it's quite the opposite; it's a step out of the dark into the light. It's not a step into the unknown. Faith is hearing what God has to say, believing it, and then acting upon it.

It's not some vague nebulous sort of thing, you're going out somewhere and you don't know what's going to happen. It's hearing what God has got to say, that's why it always comes by hearing. It's believing what God has got to say and then it's acting upon it.

Take for instance a man, who is not a Christian, he hears God saying in his word, that he, that man personally, is a sinner. Now no one else may be saying that, everybody else may be saying what a wonderful guy he is. What a wonderful woman she is, what a kind and generous person, what a lovely person, and everybody else might be saying that he is the salt of the earth. But God says he is a sinner. That is what God always says about us all.

And he believes what God has to say about him, so he comes in faith and repentance to the Lord Jesus Christ, looking for salvation, and he is saved, he is forgiven, he has peace with God. And it's all by faith.

It's faith without works. It's faith in the love and grace of God in the gospel. It's faith in what God has done and provided for him in the Lord Jesus Christ. He contributes nothing to his salvation, it's all of grace, it becomes his through faith, and he is now a Christian.

So now he is a Christian, so how does he live when he's a Christian—well he lives by faith. "Help us to walk aright, more by faith less by sight," just as the song puts it. He lives by faith. What does that mean? Well it means that he believes God as to how he is to live and behave. When he was saved he believed God that he could do nothing to contribute to his salvation. He believed God that salvation was all of grace, and he's saved. Now he believes that God adds to the quality of the life he should now live. He takes the Ten Commandments seriously. He takes the Sermon on the Mount seriously. He takes every injunction in the epistles seriously, as to how he is to live. He seeks now to live his life by faith. Only now it is faith plus works. He was saved without works, but now that he is saved, it is faith plus works, because faith without works is dead. Faith, in other words, produces action.

And isn't this the very essence of what Hebrews 11 is about? By faith Moses, didn't sit under a tree and contemplate, by faith

Moses didn't sit under a tree and twiddle his thumbs and wait for God to do something. By faith Moses refused to be called the son of Pharaoh's daughter. He did something. By faith Abraham got up and he left the Ur of the Chaldeans and he went the way that God called him. By faith Abel did certain things, and by faith Joshua fought, by faith these men acted on what God had said to them.

That's what faith is in the life of a Christian. It's believing God and its working that out in the practicalities of everyday living.

Key Verse/Passage	Hebrews 11:24-26
Main Point	The meaning of faith
Key themes	Living by faith
The 'Story'	Moses trusting God
Application	Faith motivates action

34

BECOMING A CHRISTIAN

If you are in earnest about becoming a Christian, there are a few things you need to understand.

Becoming a Christian is not like joining a club, neither is it the same as taking up a new interest or hobby. Your desire to be a Christian has to be an overwhelming necessity, and such a desire will not be created by a casual interest but only by God working in your heart and mind.

You cannot make yourself a Christian. You can decide to call yourself a Christian but that is not the same as being one. This is true because of what a Christian is. By definition a Christian is a Christ-person, one who loves the Lord Jesus Christ and seeks to live his life according to the Savior's teaching. But to do this is contrary to all that we are by nature, so our nature has to be changed if we are to be Christians, and only God can do that.

Both these points lead us to see that only God can make us Christians. This is why Paul in Ephesians 2:10 in describing himself and other believers said, "We are God's workmanship." Each Christian is the product of an extraordinary work of Almighty God. Does this mean then that there is nothing we can do and we must just wait for God to work in us? It is true that there is nothing that we can do to save ourselves but still the Bible teaches that if God is beginning to work in us, one of the first things we will notice is the growing desire to have our sins forgiven and to have peace with God. So the Bible tells us to seek the Lord.

From what we have seen so far certain things become clear.

-We need to be Christians because our sin separates us from God and will eventually take us to hell.   Sin, guilt and judgment are truths that we may not like but they are the only reasonable explanation for the state of the world today and for the state of our hearts.   These are the reasons why we need to become Christians.

-If we are to be Christians it must be in God's way and God has only one way which is through His Son, the Lord Jesus Christ. Christ is not one of many ways to God, He is the only way. That is not bigotry or intolerance, it is simply the truth.

-When Jesus died on the cross He did so to fulfil God's plan of salvation for sinners.   God made Jesus responsible for our sin and Jesus gladly accepted that awful responsibility.   So when He died on the cross He did so as a sacrifice, bearing our sin and guilt and taking the punishment for that sin.   He died in our place.   In this way God satisfies His own holiness in that our sin is dealt with legally and justly, and at the same time He is able to forgive the guilty sinner and fully pardon all our sin.

-To seek the Lord means that we acknowledge our own sin and guilt, and plead with God to save us from its consequence. This He can and will do because of what the Lord Jesus did on the cross.

-God makes us Christians by not only forgiving our sin but by also dealing with the root of the problem which is not merely our sinful behavior but our sinful nature which dictates our actions.   He changes our nature by creating in us new desires, new longings, new ambitions and new attitudes.   This is done by the power of His Holy Spirit becoming the motivating force in our lives.   When someone becomes a Christian he is a new person.   Christ now rules and reigns in his heart.

If you believe these things and you really want to become a Christian then it leaves you with only one thing to do. Trust in Christ alone to save you and hate your own sin. Plead with God to have mercy on you. Do this until you know God's peace in your heart. When you seek the Lord in this way you can be sure that He will not turn you away

Key Verse/Passage   Ephesians 2:10
Main Point   What is a Christian?
Key themes   The Christian is a new person
The 'Story'
Application   God alone makes Christians

35

WILLIAM WEBB ELLIS

The game of Rugby football traces its origin back to 1823 when a boy at Rugby School in Warwickshire while playing football picked up the ball and ran with it. Whether this story is fact or fiction it is certainly remembered today with a plaque on the wall of Rugby school and the trophy of the Rugby World Cup named the Webb Ellis Cup.

The plaque at Rugby School reads....

The great game of Rugby came about because a young boy had a 'fine disregard for the rules of football as played in his time'. So the breaking of the rules brought into existence something that has brought great pleasure to millions of people since. Breaking the rules doesn't usually have such good results and breaking God's rules certainly does not.

The difference between God's rules and any other set of rules is that they are infallible and never change. We are used to the rules of games changing from time to time; that is inevitable because we are capable of improving on something, but God always gets it right first time and his rules need no improving. Men and women find it very difficult to grasp this and think that as we can change the rules of a sport so we can change God's rules. The result of such thinking is the mess the world is in today.

When God created the world he did so meticulously and carefully, so much so that if things were only slightly different life on earth would be impossible. For example, our distance from the sun is exactly right to give earth the correct temperature to sustain human life. If the average temperature of the earth was raised by only two or three degrees, the polar ice sheets would melt and London would be under twenty feet of water. If our planet was 10% smaller or 10% larger, human life could not exist. In the same way the 23.5% tilt of the earth's axis is not some arbitrary thing but necessary for life.

Such meticulous work was needed by God to sustain human life on earth and in the same way when God planned our salvation he was equally painstaking. God's way is the only way and we cannot amend it without fatal consequences. Man is now discovering that his own foolishness and greed is affecting the ozone layer—the barrier God put forty miles above the earth to protect us from the sun's killer rays. We are all aware of the danger to life from a hole in the ozone layer. We cannot play around with God's meticulous plans either in creation or salvation. We need the cross exactly as God planned it. There can be no variation, no amendments and no changes. The cross is God's set purpose and we must accept it as such.

THE ONLY WAY
Similarly God has made a provision for our salvation. If a sinner is to be saved he needs love, grace and mercy, and these flow in abundance from the Lord Jesus Christ. The gospel is not a complicated message only understandable by theologians. It simply says that you are a sinner and Jesus is God's one and only provision for your salvation; believe the gospel; repent of your sin; have faith only in Jesus and live. But many will not do this. They rebel against the meticulously planned way of God and put their heads in a plastic bag called morality or good works or religion.

God's way is the only way but it is a sure way. God planned a perfect and foolproof way of salvation. It can save the young and the old, the clever and the dull, the rich and the poor. No one is barred from it because of race or color. That way is through the Lord Jesus Christ and is called the gospel.

God's rule for the salvation of sinners is not try your best, be religious and moral, it is believe on the Lord Jesus Christ and you shall be saved. There is no changing of that rule and we would be silly to do so. Salvation is not a game, this is a serious business with eternal consequences.

Key Verse/Passage	John 14:6
Main Point	God's rules are infallible
Key themes	God's rules are for obedience not debate
The 'Story'	The rules for Rugby
Application	Salvation is not a game

36

THE BEAUTIFUL GAME

Football is often called the beautiful game. This is sometimes difficult to see when we hear of the violence between fans at football matches. But if ever there was a beautiful football match it took place on Christmas Day in 1914. The First World War was seeing the untold slaughter of young men yet in the midst of all that a football match took place.

On January 1, 1915, the London *Times* published a letter from a major in the Medical Corps reporting that in his sector the British played a game against the Germans opposite and were beaten 3-2.

Kurt Zehmisch of the 134th Saxons recorded in his diary: 'The English brought a soccer ball from the trenches, and pretty soon a lively game ensued. How marvelously wonderful, yet how strange it was. The English officers felt the same way about it. Thus Christmas, the celebration of Love, managed to bring mortal enemies together as friends for a time.'

The Truce lasted all day; in places it ended that night, but on other sections of the line it held over Boxing Day and in some areas, a few days more. In fact, there were parts on the front where the absence of aggressive behavior was conspicuous well into 1915.

This match was not organized and the generals on both sides did not like to see their soldiers fraternizing with the enemy, so how did it happen? The answer lies in the statement above of the German soldier, 'Thus Christmas, the celebration of love,

managed to bring mortal enemies together as friends for a time.'
It is amazing what the Christmas spirit of love and peace can
achieve even in the hearts of those who are not Christians.

Men stopped trying to kill each other and instead played
football together. This is almost impossible to believe yet it
happened. True, this attitude did not last very long, but for a few
days love prevailed. What if such a spirit could last forever?
Wars would cease and family bickering would never be known.
Is that too much to hope for? Yes as long as men go on ignoring
what God has to say.

Listen to Psalm 81.
> 11 "But my people would not listen to me;
>   Israel would not submit to me.
> 12 So I gave them over to their stubborn hearts
>   to follow their own devices.
> 13 "If my people would only listen to me,
>   if Israel would only follow my ways,
> 14 how quickly I would subdue their enemies
>   and turn my hand against their foes!
> 15 Those who hate the LORD would cringe before him,
>   and their punishment would last forever.
> 16 But you would be fed with the finest of wheat;
>   with honey from the rock I would satisfy you."

SPIRITUAL HUNGER
In Psalm 81:10 we see a responsibility and a promise. The
responsibility is that we open wide our mouths and the
promise from God is that he will fill it.

The picture here is of a fledgling in a nest with their mouths
wide open to receive all the good things the parent birds have
for them. It is a picture of total dependency and intense
hunger. The word 'wide' suggests urgency, need and priority.

There is nothing half hearted about this. The mouth is wide open to grab as much as possible and to miss nothing.

This is what we are to do before the promise will be fulfilled. Almost all the great promises of scripture are conditional (1 Chronicles 7:14; Malachi 3:10; Psalm 81;10). God is sovereign and he can work without our aid but he chooses to work through his people, but this requires them to be active, not passive. He lays upon us responsibilities and demands obedience.

Come back to the fledgling in the nest. When the food goes into the mouth it provides nourishment, strength and health. God is promising this to us. He wants to fill us with all the things that will encourage and maintain spiritual growth. Is that what you want? Are you fed up with your own base desires? Are you weary with how sin and the world so appeal to you? When our life is saturated with God then assurance, enjoyment and satisfaction abound. It does not mean there will be no more problems but v. 14 will then become a reality.

There is so much for us in Christ so why do we live on bread and water when there is a banqueting table available. How do we open our mouths wide? By using the means of grace— prayer, the Bible and fellowship. We need to stop waiting for something to happen and instead take the initiative in response to God's promise.

Key Verse/Passage	Psalm 81
Main Point	Open wide your mouth
Key themes	Using the means of grace
The 'Story'	The Football Game during the war
Application	Conditional promises

37

THE HAND OF GOD

Argentina vs. England, played on 22 June 1986, was a football match in the quarter-finals of the 1986 FIFA World Cup at the Estadio Azteca in Mexico City. The game was held four years after the Falklands War between Argentina and the United Kingdom and was a key part in developing the intense football rivalry between the two nations. It was also a match which included two of the most famous goals in football history, both scored by Diego Maradona. His first, after fifty-one minutes, was the *Hand of God goal*, in which Maradona scored with an illegal, but unpenalised, handball. His second, after fifty-four minutes, saw him dribble past six England players.

Maradona claimed that it was not his hand which knocked the ball into the English net but it was the hand of God. Of course no one believed him but it does raise the question, does God intervene in the affairs of men, especially in only a game? The Bible has no doubt that God does intervene from time to time and we call these interventions, miracles.

Joshua 10 relates one of the most remarkable miracles recorded in Scripture. By definition any miracle is remarkable, but for the sun to stand still seems more amazing than anything. Pink defines a miracle as a 'supernatural event brought about by a special act of divine providence, an extraordinary display of God's power. It is an event occurring in the natural world, which is apparent to the senses and of such a nature that it can be rationally attributed only to an immediate act of God.'

Christianity is a supernatural faith; therefore we should not be surprised to read in the Bible of miracles. But these remarkable and exceptional acts of God that so baffle and defy human reason are not found everywhere in Scripture. John MacArthur writes, 'Most biblical miracles happened in three relatively brief periods of Bible history: in the days of Moses and Joshua, during the ministries of Elijah and Elisha, and in the time of Christ and the apostles. None of these periods lasted much more than a hundred years. Each of them saw a proliferation of miracles unheard of in other eras. Even during those three time periods, however, miracles were not exactly the order of the day. The miracles that happened involved men who were extraordinary messengers from God—Moses and Joshua, Elijah and Elisha, Jesus and the apostles.'

In Scripture there are a few other isolated incidents of the miraculous. This has to be borne in mind today when you hear some Christians talk of miracles as if they are as common as a loaf of bread. I remember a few years ago seeing a large notice outside a church which read, 'Come in, there is a miracle waiting for you.' On the other hand there are Christians who do not believe that miracles are possible today. They argue that they finished at the end of the apostolic era. So even among Christians the subject can be contentious, but what every Bible believing Christian has no doubt about is that the miracles recorded in Scripture actually happened.

Miracles remind man that he is not as clever as he thinks he is and they reveal the supreme glory and power of God. Once we accept the fact of a sovereign, omnipotent God, it is not difficult to believe in miracles.

Key Verse/Passage	Matthew 19:26
Main Point	What is a miracle?
Key themes	Does God still intervene in our affairs?
The 'Story'	The Goal called *The Hand of God*
Application	Have you ever seen a miracle?

38

OUT FOR A DUCK

Cricket is explained in the following:
You have two sides, one out in the field and one in. Each man that's in the side that's in goes out, and when he's out he comes in and the next man goes in until he's out. When they are all out, the side that's out comes in and the side that's been in goes out and tries to get those coming in, out. Sometimes you get men still in and not out.
When a man goes out to go in, the men who are out try to get him out, and when he is out he goes in and the next man in goes out and goes in. There are two men called umpires who stay out all the time and they decide when the men who are in are out.
When both sides have been in and all the men have been out, and both sides have been out twice after all the men have been in, including those who are not out, that is the end of the game.
Permalink, Tea Towel Explanation of Cricket

Cricket is a game you either love or hate. The above well known description of the game reveals how absurd it is to those who do not understand it. Many though love it passionately and follow it keenly. A cricket match can be set to take 5 days but still end up as a draw. Strange! Cricket has its own vocabulary with maiden overs, googlies, silly mid on, lbw, out for a duck, etc. You have to love it or hate it.

The Australians love it and particularly they love nothing better than beating England at cricket. This they did regularly during the career of Don Bradman. Bradman was the greatest batsman that Australia ever produced. He had a batting average in test matches of 99.9. He played his last test at the Oval in London in 1948 needing only 4 runs to achieve a test average 100, but he was out without scoring.

It's amazing that the great Don Bradman could get a duck (out without scoring). Even the great can fail and it reminds us that we can expect too much from people. But in the end in sport does it really matter? After all it's only a game and who today, apart from cricket buffs, remembers Bradman's batting averages?

Failure in the Christian life is something else. Unless it is dealt with it can have ongoing repercussions. Have you failed in some aspect of your Christian life? If so, you must learn from that failure. Find out where you went wrong, and determine not to do the same thing again. The devil intends to use failure to dishearten you, but by the grace of God you can use it as a springboard to victory. Let your failure teach you your need of complete dependence upon Jesus Christ (John 15:1-5).

In the Old Testament, Ebenezer was the place of Israel's greatest failure, and also the place of a great victory. At Ebenezer the people of God lost the Ark of the Covenant to their enemies the Philistines (read 1 Samuel 4:1-22). Here was terrible failure, and it was the direct result of neglecting the things of God. Read now chapter 7 of 1 Samuel and see how Ebenezer (v. 12) became the place of victory. It was the same God, the same place, the same people, the same enemy; yet instead of defeat and failure there was victory. Why?

v. 2 they lamented after the Lord—they wanted God, they cried to God with earnestness and urgency.

vv. 3-6 they repented of the sin that had caused defeat and failure.

v. 8 they put their trust in the Lord, and in him alone. The result was that all that had been lost was restored (vv. 13-14).

The next time you fail, remember Ebenezer!

> *Here I raise my Ebenezer,*
> *Hither by Thy help I'm come,*
> *And I hope by Thy good pleasure*
> *Safely to arrive at home ...*
> *Prone to wander, Lord, I feel it,*
> *Prone to leave the God I love;*
> *Take my heart, O take and seal it,*
> *Seal it from Thy courts above!*
>   -Robert Robinson

Key Verse/Passage	John 15:1-5
Main Point	How to deal with failure
Key themes	Learning from our failures
The 'Story'	The failure of the greatest batsman
Application	What turned failure into victory at Ebenezer?

39

"YOU CANNOT BE SERIOUS!"

John Patrick McEnroe, Jr. (born February 16, 1959) is a former World No. 1 professional tennis player from the United States. During his career, he won seven Grand Slam singles titles (three at Wimbledon and four at the US Open), nine Grand Slam men's doubles titles, and one Grand Slam mixed doubles title. McEnroe also won a record eight season ending championships, comprising five WCT Finals titles and three Masters Grand Prix titles from twelve final appearances at these two events, a record he shares with Ivan Lendl. In addition he won 19 Championship Series top tier events of the Grand Prix Tour that were the precursors to the current Masters 1000.

He is best remembered for his shot-making artistry and superb volleying; for his famous rivalries with Björn Borg, Jimmy Connors and Ivan Lendl; for his confrontational on-court behavior which frequently landed him in trouble with umpires and tennis authorities; and for the catchphrase "You cannot be serious!" directed toward an umpire during a match at Wimbledon in 1981. (Wikipedia)

'You cannot be serious' was McEnroe's complaint against the umpire who called one of his shots out. He could not believe what was happening and his tantrum got him into hot water with Wimbledon officials. For someone to be amazed at someone else's opinion is not unusual but the reaction of angry tantrum is never justified.

When Saul of Tarsus was converted and became a Christian, other believers were astonished. They said, 'All those who heard him were astonished and asked, "Isn't he the man who raised havoc in Jerusalem among those who call on this name? And hasn't he come here to take them as prisoners to the chief priests?" They must have said something like 'you cannot be serious' to the messenger who brought the news to them. The depth of divine grace can take even believers by surprise. The history of the church is full of incidents of surprising conversions when the least expected become Christians. Charles Spurgeon once said that ex-poachers make the best gamekeepers, and the Lord often does exactly that.

John Newton made his living in the slave trade. At 23 years of age he was a foul mouth hardened sinner with no thought of God, but circumstances brought him to fear death. He began to read the Bible and to seek God. Anyone who knew this man would have found this unbelievable. 'You can't be serious,' would have been their response. But it was true and John Newton became a Christian, a preacher of the gospel and the writer of the great hymn *Amazing Grace*.

What would you think of a man with a vicious temper who once when his dog displeased him cut off the animals head with a bread knife. His contemporaries would avoid him because of his filthy language and general unpleasantness. Could such a man ever be saved? The answer has to be no, especially when he has reached the age if seventy in such a state. If salvation was anything but by grace it would have been totally impossible.

That same night 'Staffordshire Bill' passed from condemnation to life. 'He found,' Mrs. Lloyd-Jones tells us, 'that he could understand the things that were being said, he believed the gospel and his heart was flooded with a great peace. Old things had passed away, all things had become new. The transformation in his face was remarkable, it had the radiance of a saint. As he walked out that night with another man, they passed me, and the man said, "Mrs. Jones, this is Staffordshire Bill." I shall never forget the agonized look on his face, for he flinched as though he had been struck a sudden blow. "Oh no, oh no," he said, "that's a bad old name for a bad man; I am William Thomas now.'"

God has a habit of doing things that cause us to say, 'You can't be serious'. He amazes us by his grace and love. He says, in Isaiah 55:8, 'For my thoughts are not your thoughts, neither are your ways my ways.'

John Newton used to say that when he gets to heaven he will have three surprises,
the first will be that there will be those there he never expected,
the second will be that people he expected to be there are not there,
and the biggest surprise of all is that he is there.

Key Verse/Passage	Isaiah 55:8
Main Point	Why is grace amazing?
Key themes	God's surprising actions
The 'Story'	John McEnroe's startled cry
Application	Have you ever been surprised by God?

40

INGA THE WINGER

Widely known as 'Inga the Winger', Va'aiga Lealuga Tuigamala is also known as being one of the most powerful, hard-hitting and versatile backs ever to play the game of rugby. Despite his ferociously physical approach on the field, Inga is also well known for his devotion to the Christian faith, and in particular for the influence he had with future England rugby union captain Jason Robinson, a team-mate at Wigan. Over their months of friendship, Tuigamala shared his Christian faith, and is credited as being a key influence in Robinson's conversion and resurrection as a man and player.

Next to the preaching of the gospel, the thing that God uses most in the saving of souls is the witness of friends and loved ones. This unorganized evangelism is one of the most effective ways of reaching sinners with the gospel. Tuigamala's influence upon Jason Robinson, and probably many others, can never be over estimated.

In the Old Testament in 2 Kings 5 we read the story of the healing of Naaman. Naaman had much going for him (v. 1), but he was a leper and this cancelled out everything else. His life was grinding to a standstill but help came from an unexpected quarter (vv. 2-3). This nameless girl bore a faithful testimony to the power of God to heal through his servant Elisha. The witness of the girl ought to be an encouragement to us all. In the most difficult of circumstances—she had been taken from her family and home and now was a slave in a foreign land—she bore testimony to the goodness of God. And the significant thing is that the general, his wife and the king (vv. 4-5) followed the girl's advice. She must have made a great impression upon them with regard to the reality of her faith, otherwise Naaman would not have listened to her.

Successful witness is not only a matter of saying the right thing, but also involves living a life that gives substance to our words.

In the Queen's birthday honors of 2008 Tuigamala was appointed to the Order of New Zealand. But I wonder what honor God will bestow upon this man for his faithful witness. Certainly like all faithful believers he will receive the order of 'Well done, good and faithful servant! You have been faithful with a few things; I will put you in charge of many things. Come and share your master's happiness!' (Matthew 25:21,23).

Many believers find personal witness very difficult whilst others find it as easy as pie. I remember many years ago being at a minister's conference and at the end of the day a crowd of us went into the village for a bag of chips. As we were waiting in the queue at the chip shop the shop keeper asked where we were all from, a friend of mine standing at the beginning of the queue, answered without a moment's hesitation, 'it does not matter where we are from, it is where we are going that is important'. And immediately he was telling the shop keeper about Jesus. I don't think I could have done that but to my friend it was a natural response.

How we witness is not important but *that* we witness is.

The last recorded words of the risen Christ to his apostles before his ascension were, 'you will be my witnesses ...'. Every Christian is called to be a witness.

WITNESSING BEGINS WITH CARING
It begins, firstly, with caring about *the glory of God.* God is not glorified and honored in this world because the vast majority of people do not know and love him. His truth is trampled in the

mud and his name is constantly taken in vain. The only way for this to change is for people to become Christians. Look at how different your attitude to God is now, compared to what it was before you were converted. If you care enough about God's glory, you will tell people the good news of the gospel.

Witnessing begins, secondly, with caring about *people,* caring about unbelievers in their bondage and spiritual blindness. Without Christ, men and women are going to hell. Do you care? Then witness to them of the only way of effective salvation. Many Christians are timid about witnessing. To counteract this a great many different methods and schemes of personal evangelism have been devised. This is all done with the best of intentions, but it does not provide the answer to the problem. It makes witnessing too mechanical and artificial, so that instead of being a natural overflow, it becomes rather like scraping the bottom of the barrel.

To become a faithful witness we must begin with obedience to the two greatest commandments. We must love the Lord our God, and we must love our neighbor as ourselves. It is such people who will be blessed by God in all that they do.

Key Verse/Passage	Acts 1:8
Main Point	Why was Namaan's maid so effective?
Key themes	Why was Inga's witness effective
The 'Story'	2 Kings 5
Application	How can I be a good witness?

41

VIDEO REF

Many sports today are using video refs to decide disputed scores. For instance in rugby if the actual referee cannot be sure if a try has been scored he will go to the video ref for a decision. The video ref sits up in the stand with a TV screen for instant replay or slow motion to help come to a conclusion. This has been helpful even if it is not always accurate. Sometimes the outcome of a game can rest upon what the video ref says.

God does not need video replays to decide if man has sinned. Very often men try to fool God but it never works. One of the most terrible effects of sin in the human heart and mind is that it deludes us in just about every aspect of our understanding about God. The greatest delusion of all is to believe that there is no God, and that seems to be becoming a more popular opinion at the beginning of the twenty-first century.

But even those who say they believe in God may be subject to a delusion. We imagine we can reduce God to a size we can manipulate and control. One result of this is to think we can treat God in the same way as we treat each other. We can fool and deceive each other; so it follows that we can fool God. A 'God' whom we can deceive, and from whom we can hide things, is no God at all. The reality is that there is a God and that he cannot be fooled by us. He sees and knows all things. So what we consider to be secret sins are, as far as God is concerned, committed with blazing publicity.

Another delusion is that it is permissible to amend the laws of God, so that what the Bible considers to be sin is no longer regarded as sin by the modern mind. We modernize what God has said in order to soothe our consciences, but that does not change the fact that sin is still sin.

These delusions, and others, will one day be shown up for what they are and we shall have a rude awakening when God confronts us with our twisted beliefs and actions. The omniscient God is not fooled by our pretences. He knows all things and sees all things and he certainly knows the nature of man. Sporting referees are only human and even with the help of the video ref they sometimes get it wrong, but God never gets it wrong. That's a very solemn thought—God never gets it wrong. It leaves us in a position of never being able to pull the wool over God's eyes; we can never deceive him and our sin is ever open before him.

Key Verse/Passage	Hebrews 4:13
Main Point	God never gets it wrong
Key themes	The all wise and all knowing God
The 'Story'	A call on the field overturned by the video ref
Application	You cannot deceive God

42

COUNTERFEIT TICKETS

Think of a great sporting event that takes place each year. The demand for tickets to see this event is enormous, and every year we hear of counterfeit tickets being sold. These are very much like the official tickets, but they are false; they do not carry the authority of the sport's governing body. It is easy to imagine an avid fan buying one of these counterfeit tickets, believing it to be genuine and that it guarantees him a seat for the big match. With great expectation he travels hundreds of miles to the stadium, only to be turned away at the gate.

His sincerity, and his absolute confidence that the ticket was genuine, are of no avail at all. He has been deceived. There is no entrance for him.

Satan is the great deceiver. He is an expert at producing counterfeit ways of salvation. Be careful. Be sure that your hope rests in the way God himself has prepared for sinners. It is God's remedy for sin that you need, not your own.

People resent being told that they are sinners. They will admit that they are not perfect, but think they are not too bad really— as good as most people, they like to believe, and better than some. The tendency therefore is to treat sin and its consequences lightly, and it is an easy step from there for man to think that he can provide his own remedy for sin.

Let us take a few minutes to consider some of the remedies people argue for:

GOOD WORKS
But what does God's Word say about good works and morality as a remedy for sin and a means of salvation? 'All our righteous acts are like filthy rags' (Isaiah 64:6). 'For it is by grace that you have been saved, through faith ...not by works, so that no one can boast' (Ephesians 2:8).

Try your best, say some. Be kind. Be helpful. Be interested in some charity and work hard for it. This is the way to be sure of gaining heaven.

MORALITY
For others the answer is: be honest and true. Do not lie or cheat. Do not be immoral in any way. Surely God cannot expect more than that of any man!

Good works and morality are to be commended, but they cannot put sin right. They cannot take away God's anger and they cannot save your soul. Rather, the words of Paul, the former Pharisee, express it well, 'He saved us, not because of righteous things we had done, but because of his mercy' (Titus 3:5).

RELIGION
According to others the remedy for sin must surely lie in religion. Go to church. Be faithful and devout. Say your prayers. Give to the poor.

Once again, these things are good and highly commendable, but they are only another form of good works and morality. The problem of sin remains unanswered. Read the story in Mark 10:17-27 of the man who was good, moral and religious, but had no salvation and no eternal life.

There are many people who believe in all sincerity that their remedies for sin are good enough, and that these things will most surely earn them a place in heaven.

Jesus warns us of this in the Sermon on the Mount,
"Not everyone who says to me, 'Lord, Lord,' will enter the kingdom of heaven, but only the one who does the will of my Father who is in heaven. Many will say to me on that day, 'Lord, Lord, did we not prophesy in your name and in your name drive out demons and in your name perform many miracles?' Then I will tell them plainly, 'I never knew you. Away from me, you evildoers!' (Matthew 7:21-23).

The same warning is given in Proverbs 14:12, *"There is a way that appears to be right, but in the end it leads to death."*

THE ONLY REMEDY FOR SIN IS GOD'S REMEDY.
'For God so loved the world that he gave his one and only Son, that whoever believes in him shall not perish but have eternal life' (John 3:16).

Here we have a perfect statement of God's glorious remedy for sin. God hates sin, but in his divine love he has prepared a remedy which deals justly with the punishment that sin deserves, and yet at the same time provides pardon for the sinner. The sacrificial death of Jesus Christ is our only remedy.

When you buy a ticket for a big match you do not expect to get a counterfeit. You naturally assume you are buying the genuine article. But let us imagine you are taken in, what are the consequences of this? You will have lost your money and you do not see the match. If you are taken in on the matter of an entrance into heaven this means you will spend eternity in hell. So you had better be sure. You cannot afford to be wrong.

Key Verse/Passage	Proverbs 14:12
Main Point	Man's deceptions
Key themes	God's perfect remedy
The 'Story'	Counterfeit tickets do not gain entrance
Application	Be sure you have the only right remedy

43

ENGLAND'S RUGBY WORLD CUP

When England won the Rugby World Cup in 2003, in an unprecedented move, every member of England's Rugby World Cup-winning side, plus coaches Clive Woodward, Dave Alfred, Phil Larder and Andy Robinson were recognized in the New Year Honors list.

Nations love to honor their heroes, especially their sporting heroes. When the triumph comes around so rarely this honor becomes more extreme.

The Christian could learn from this and perhaps give more honor and praise to our 'hero', the Lord Jesus Christ. Jesus has won for us not merely a sporting trophy, but eternal life. Isn't this something to shout about? It is amazing that believers are so reluctant to talk about Jesus. We seem willing to talk about anything and everything except Jesus. Perhaps this is because we have never fully understood what the Lord has done for us.

Every Christian was once a guilty sinner going to hell, but now he is a child of God. It is Jesus alone who has achieved this for us. That is staggering; it is almost unbelievable, but none the less that is exactly what it means to be a Christian. This is so glorious that we need to tell people about it. What are we to tell them? We are to tell them about Jesus.

WHO IS JESUS?
Jesus is God. God reveals himself in Scripture as God the Father, God the Son, and God the Holy Spirit. This is called the

Trinity. There are not three separate Gods, but one God. This is a great mystery: none the less it is a fact.

The New Testament leaves us in no doubt as to who Jesus is. 'He is the image of the invisible God, the firstborn over all creation. For by him all things were created' (Colossians 1:15, 16). 'For God was pleased to have all his fullness dwell in him' (1:19). 'For in Christ all the fullness of the Deity lives in bodily form' (2:9). 'The Son is the radiance of God's glory and the exact representation of his being' (Hebrews 1:3).

In the Old Testament the prophet Isaiah was given a remarkable revelation of the glory and holiness of God. He sees and hears the angelic host crying, 'Holy, holy, holy is the Lord Almighty; the whole earth is full of his glory' (Isaiah 6:3). The prophet himself says, 'My eyes have seen the King, the Lord Almighty' (verse 5). In the New Testament the apostle John refers to this incident and says, 'Isaiah said this because he saw Jesus' glory and spoke about him' (John 12:41). Jesus is the holy God the angels spoke of. Jesus is the King, the Lord Almighty, whom Isaiah saw. Jesus is God.

The good news (the 'gospel') is that when Jesus Christ died on the cross, 'he bore the sin of many' and saved them from God's anger against sin and the judgment they deserve. He alone was innocent of sin and could act as a substitute—he stood in our place and took the punishment his people deserved. He died, 'the righteous for the unrighteous, to bring us to God' (1 Peter 3:18). By his death he not only turns away God's anger, but also reconciles to God all that the Father has given him.

Jesus is God's way of salvation, which is why he is the only way.

This is of more than passing interest. It is crucial for our salvation. Jesus came to make atonement for our sin. That meant he had to die in our place, for that was the penalty God had decreed for sin. He came therefore to die as a sacrifice for us; to die in our stead. That was God's plan: 'He was pierced for our transgressions, he was crushed for our iniquities; the punishment that brought us peace was upon him, and by his wounds we are healed' (Isaiah 53:5).

But in order to do this Jesus had to be sinless, so that death should have no rightful claims on him. The slightest sin in Jesus would have made him no different from all other men, and would have been sufficient to bring upon him the penalty of death. He would then have to die for his own sins; in no way could he have offered to die instead of us. But, thank God, only hours before he was crucified, he was able to say, 'The prince of this world [the devil] is coming. He has no hold on me' John 14:30). What Jesus was saying was that the devil had no claim upon him at all. The sinlessness of the Savior deprived the devil of any authority or control over him. More than that, it made it impossible for the Evil One to make any lawful demands upon Jesus and so Almighty God, the Lord Jesus Christ, was able to die for our sins.

Key Verse/Passage	Colossians 2:9
Main Point	Who is Jesus?
Key themes	What would you tell a sinner about Jesus?
The 'Story'	The shallowness of earthly heroes
Application	There is no one like Jesus

44

A HOLE IN ONE

It is amazing how the game of golf can take over some men. They start playing for a little exercise and before long are addicts. They can't get enough of the little white ball. I was never like that but I did like to play this amazing game. Mind you, I was never very good and my game varied between poor and pathetic. I remember once playing in Coventry and hooking three successive balls way off to the left and into a river. What with the price of golf balls that was an expensive round. I lined up to drive my fourth ball rather anxiously but it flew straight and all my hooks were forgotten. No wonder some people call golf a good walk spoilt by a golf ball.

On one course we came to a 172 yard par 3 hole. This meant it was 172 yards from the tee to the hole and the chaps who were supposed to know said it should take three shots to get the ball in the hole. I never seemed to agree with these chaps who set the pars and par 3 for me meant about 5 shots. I mean, hitting a 4.25 inch target from 172 yards by smacking a small ball with a golf club is no easy task. Like all golfers I dreamt of getting a hole in one, but that would only be if pigs could fly.

That day my drive off the tee was unusually excellent and the ball soared off towards the 4.25 hole. When we got up to the green I was amazed to see my ball only 12 inches from the hole. I was exhilarated and disappointed. Exhilarated because it was the best golf shot I had ever hit, and disappointed because it was only 12 inches away from the rare hole in one. If only it had rolled another 12 inches but no it was no hole in one ... so near yet so far. A hole in two is good but not good enough. My very best was still short of the mark.

There are many people like that with God... so near and yet so far. They are not bad people and not atheists, but they are not Christians. There were some people in the New Testament like that. A man named Agrippa said he was almost persuaded to be a Christian. Sadly almost is not enough. He may as well have been a 100 miles away.

There was a young man who came to Jesus asking the right questions and in the right spirit. He was very near to God, but when Jesus confronted him with his obsessive love of money, he went away from Jesus sad. So near yet so far.

What about you? You may be very religious and quite a moral person, but are you a real Christian? Do you know the Lord Jesus Christ as your Savior? Jesus said that there is only one way to become a Christian and that is to be born again.

Jesus said in John 3, you must be born again.

How Do We Become Born Again?

To answer this let us consider 1 Peter 1:23-25, "For you have been born again, not of perishable seed, but of imperishable' through the living and enduring word of God. For, 'All men are like grass, and all their glory is like the flowers of the field; the grass withers and the flowers fall, but the word of the Lord stands for ever.' Peter also parallels physical and spiritual birth. How does physical birth come about? By the planting of man's seed in a woman. Peter calls this perishable seed. It will not last forever. Spiritual birth also needs a seed to be planted. This seed is the imperishable word of God, which (v. 25) lasts forever. The implanting comes via the preaching of the Word. This is how God works new birth. He brings sinners under the sound of the Word. "Faith comes through hearing the message" (Romans 10:17). The Gospel shows us our true condition. All have sinned, the good respectable people and the moral outcasts. The Word convinces us that we need to be born again. Only in the Word of God are we shown what God has done in and through the Lord Jesus Christ to deal with our sin.

So if a man wants to be born again, he must go to the Word of God. He must read it, hear it preached and obey it. The Word will turn the seeker of new life in God, to Jesus the only Savior.

While you are not likely to ever get a hole in one at golf, you can be born again when you come to Jesus in faith and repentance.

Key Verse/Passage	Mark 14:34
Main Point	Why is almost persuaded not enough?
Key themes	You must be born again
The 'Story'	Coming close to a hole in one
Application	Why is the Bible essential to being born again?

45

JOIN THE LIBRARY

Thousands of folk visit their local library every week. It costs nothing and there are thousands of books to choose from. There is another library that has only 66 books but it is the best library in the world. It is called the BIBLE. The word Bible means library.

The word 'Bible' comes from the Greek word *biblia,* meaning 'books'. The Bible is a collection of sixty-six books. Thirty-nine of them, which we call the Old Testament, were written originally in Hebrew (with a few short passages in Aramaic). The other twenty-seven, which are known as the New Testament, were written in Greek. These books were written by about forty men over a period of 1,500 years. Clearly, the original manuscripts would not last forever, and so they had to be copied. The men who copied them were called scribes.

We can say then that these early scribes took great care to ensure that their copying was accurate, even counting every letter of every book to check that not one had been left out. As a matter of fact, the Hebrew word for 'scribe' originally meant 'to count'.

During the 1,500 years that the Bible was being written, many other books were written for which some sort of authority was claimed. In the Old Testament era, for instance, there were the books of the Apocrypha, and in the New Testament era there were writings such as *The Shepherd of Hermas* and *The Epistle of Barnabas.* Why are these not included in our Bible? And how were those sixty-six books chosen for inclusion in what we regard as the inspired Scriptures?

THE OLD TESTAMENT
There is an old Jewish tradition that it was Ezra who first compiled the Old Testament canon, even though there were collections of the first five books (known as the Pentateuch) and some of the prophets long before his time. We can never be sure how these thirty nine books were put together, but we know that by the time Jesus was born the books of the Old Testament had been agreed upon.

The books of the Jewish Old Testament were divided into three groups—the Law, the Prophets and the Writings. *The Law* consisted of the five books written by Moses: Genesis, Exodus, Leviticus, Numbers and Deuteronomy. *The Prophets* included Joshua, Judges, Samuel, Kings, Isaiah, Jeremiah, Ezekiel, and also the prophets from Hosea to Malachi in our Bible today. *The Writings* were Psalms, Proverbs, Job, Song of Solomon, Ruth, Lamentations, Ecclesiastes, Esther, Daniel, Ezra, Nehemiah and Chronicles.

The order of the books in our English Bible is that of the Septuagint, a Greek translation of the Old Testament made in the second century BC. The Bible that Jesus used and so often referred to is our Old Testament, and most of its thirty-nine books are quoted in the New Testament.

THE NEW TESTAMENT
Most of the twenty-seven New Testament books were written within forty years of the death of Jesus, and all of them within seventy years, but it was not until AD 397 that the canon was finally agreed.

It is clear from the New Testament itself that the early church regarded the thirty-nine Old Testament books as the Word of God. They are repeatedly quoted in the New Testament as authoritative. But to give complete expression to the Christian faith, more than this was needed. At first, of course, the apostles would be able to give a spoken testimony to the truth; but after their death a written record was required. So God in His goodness gave the church the New Testament. By the close of the second century, the four Gospels (Matthew, Mark, Luke and John), together with the book of Acts, were commonly regarded as the early authentic history of Christ and His church.

There is little doubt that by this time also the thirteen epistles of Paul were accepted as inspired. In fact, most of the twenty-seven New Testament books were generally accepted by Christians; but there was hesitation over a few of them including James, Jude and 2 Peter. Besides this, many other books were circulating among the churches. The situation needed clarification, and so the churches of the West gathered at Carthage in AD 397 and settled the content of the New Testament once and for all. Two tests were applied to the many books in circulation. Did the book come from the time of the apostles? And did its teaching agree with known apostolic doctrine?

'It is clear that the New Testament canon was not the result of ecclesiastical pronouncements, but grew in accordance with the needs of the church. The major factor governing selection was 'apostolicity'—the conviction that the books represented the position of the apostolic age." Donald Guthrie

Join the library and read all 66 of its books.

Key Verse/Passage	2 Timothy 3:16
Main Point	You can trust your Bible
Key themes	2 Peter 1: 20-21
The 'Story'	The story of the forming of the canon
Application	1 Peter 2: 1-2

46

A FAVORITE HYMN

Most Christians have a favourite hymn. It may be the tune or the words that appeal to them but either way they love to sing it. My favourite was written in the 18th century by a man with the posh name of Augustus Montague Toplady. The hymn is titled *A Debtor to Mercy Alone*.

1. A DEBTOR to mercy alone,
Of covenant mercy I sing;
Nor fear, with Thy righteousness on,
My person and offering to bring;
The terrors of law and of God
With me can have nothing to do;
My Savior's obedience and blood
Hide all my transgressions from view.

2. The work which His goodness began,
The arm of His strength will complete;
His promise is Yea and Amen,
And never was forfeited yet.
Things future, nor things that are now,
Not all things below nor above,
Can make Him His purpose forgo,
Or sever my soul from His love.

3. My name from the palms of His hands
Eternity will not erase;
Impressed on His heart it remains,
In marks of indelible grace;
Yes, I to the end shall endure,
As sure as the earnest is given;
More happy, but not more secure,
The glorified spirits in heaven.

The last verse is a glorious testimony to the salvation God himself has instigated. *Marks of indelible grace* is an amazing description of the eternal value of this work of God. How else could we have the confidence of enduring to the end? The last two lines are a wondrous testimony to once saved, saved forever. The saints in heaven are "more happy" than those still struggling in this world, but they are not "more secure."

Grace is the amazing message that God has done all that is necessary in and through the Lord Jesus Christ to save sinners. The grace of God is the most thrilling concept that can occupy the mind of a Christian, and when it occupies the mind it will soon flood the heart with praise to God that such a thing exists. Without grace there is no hope for any of us. The only alternative to grace is salvation by our own efforts. This is a non-starter because God will not accept it. The New Testament makes that abundantly clears. If salvation is to be effective it has to be acceptable to God. This is why grace is the key word in the gospel, because it delights in the Lord Jesus Christ as the sacrifice which God himself has provided. If we do not understand the New Testament meaning of the word grace, we will never understand the gospel, because grace is the key to understanding the substance and heart of its message, which is salvation through Christ alone.

A few years ago I received an invitation to preach in California. As the time drew near for my departure I grew somewhat concerned because I had not received a ticket from the churches who had invited me to preach. But they were soon on the phone telling me not to worry because I did not need a ticket. This did not relieve my concern, rather it deepened it. Of course I needed a ticket. Everyone knows you cannot fly without a ticket. What on earth were those folk in California talking about?

They then started to explain to me something called electronic ticketing. Apparently all I had to do was to present myself at the airlines desk at Heathrow Airport, tell them who I was, show them my passport and they would then give me a ticket.

I had never heard of this before and I was rather dubious. I wanted the comfort of a ticket in my hand before I left home. They again had to reassure me that it would be all right. 'It has all been taken care of at this end,' they said.

Of course, all my fears were unfounded. It had all been taken care of at the other end, the folk inviting me knew it, and the airline knew it, even if I was a bit uncertain.

The grace of God is something like that—it has all been taken care of at the other end.

One day I will set out on the most important journey any one can take—from this life to the next. I will have to stand before God and he will say, 'who are you?' I will answer by giving him my name.

'O, yes,' God will reply, 'you are the one my Son died for and paid the debt for your sins; you are the one Jesus loved and saved. Come on into heaven, you are welcome because of what Jesus has done for you.'

Salvation is all taken care of by Jesus the Savior. This is a great comfort to a sinner like myself who is always full of doubts and uncertainties.

Has Jesus taken care of your salvation?

Key Verse/Passage	Psalm 122
Main Point	Worship is the chief end of man
Key themes	Do our hymns give us a sense of God?
The 'Story'	A favorite hymn celebrating mercy
Application	What are more important in a hymn, the words or the tune. Explain.

47

ONE GOSPEL

In Galatians chapter 1 Paul tells us that there is only one gospel.

How a person becomes a Christian is obviously of prime importance. In verse three, Paul very simply tells us that it is through "the Lord Jesus Christ, who gave himself for our sins and rescued us from the present evil age." This is the gospel. This is God's way of salvation. It involves the atoning death of Jesus as our substitute on the cross (he gave himself for our sins), and the justifying redemptive work of grace (he rescued us). This and nothing else can save a guilty sinner.

It was this gospel that Paul preached to the Galatians when he visited their cities on his first missionary journey in AD 47 (Acts 13-14). They believed and were saved but soon after some Jews, who claimed to be Christians, came to them with a 'different gospel' (verse 6), which said that grace alone was not enough and circumcision was also necessary for salvation (Acts 15:1). Paul was not surprised that another way of salvation was being preached because the devil was always trying that, but he was astonished that the Galatians had believed it.

There is only one gospel. Anything else is a different gospel, indeed it is no gospel at all because it distorts the good news of God's free gift of salvation in Christ. It is a 'perverted gospel' (verse 7) in that it may sound like the real thing and will speak of Jesus, but it keeps souls away from God and does not open up to them the divine plan of salvation. If you are a young Christian it is almost certain that your doctrinal roots have not had time to grow very deep. Therefore you too can be vulnerable to a different gospel.

Any message that tells you that the grace of God in Jesus Christ is not enough to save you, but that you also need something else, is to be shunned as poison for your soul. You do not need the grace of God plus circumcision to be saved. You do not need the grace of God plus speaking in tongues to be saved. There is no plus that needs to be added to the grace of God. For you, with a four inch paint brush in your hand, to try to add a few improving touches to a masterpiece by Leonardo de Vinci, would be reasonable compared to trying to add to the grace of God.

Grace is needed because of both the character of man and the character of God. Though man was created in the image of God, able to know and enjoy him, when man sinned he was separated from God, and sin has since dominated all his actions. He is now alien to God his Maker and, because of his sinful character, he can do nothing about it. God's character on the other hand is such that he cannot condone or overlook sin. His holiness, truth and justice demand that man must be dealt with as he is, and that sin must be punished.

These two factors, taken on their own, would condemn all men to an eternity in hell. But God's character is also such that, though he hates sin, he loves the guilty sinner who deserves his judgment. Divine love therefore plans salvation, and divine grace provides salvation. Grace is the free, unmerited, undeserved favor of God to sinners.

In the seventeenth century, a Scottish preacher named James Dickson said that he had taken all his bad deeds and put them in a heap, and taken all his good deeds and put them in another heap, and fled from them both to Jesus. That is what faith in the grace of God looks like. Is that what *you* have done?

Key Verse/Passage   Galatians 1:6-10
Main Point   What is the gospel?
Key themes   What is a perverted gospel
The 'Story'
Application   Is one gospel enough?

48

SUPERSTAR

In 2012 Andrew Lloyd Webber was looking for a new Jesus to play the lead role in his new production of Jesus Christ Superstar. It should not be too difficult to find one because there is nothing special about the Jesus of Superstar. He was not born of a virgin, he was not sinless, he was not the Son of God, he did not die for sinners and he did not rise from the dead. In fact he bears no resemblance to the real Jesus. Superstar may be good entertainment but the Jesus of the New Testament was no entertainer, he was the Savior.

It is not a new Jesus we want but the Jesus God sent into this world to be our Savior. The world today needs Jesus because he is the only one who can deal with the problem of sin and it is human sin that lies at the heart of the misery and despair that fills the lives of men and women.

Jesus is God. Whereas many find it difficult to believe this and some who call themselves Christians even deny it, the fact is that this is what Jesus believed and this is what the Bible clearly teaches.

Everything about the Christian faith hinges on this. C. S. Lewis, in *Mere Christianity* said, 'You must make your choice. Either this man was, and is, the Son of God; or else a mad man or something worse. You can shut him up for a fool; you can spit at him and kill him for a demon; or you can fall at his feet and call him Lord and God. But let us not come with any patronizing nonsense about him being a great human teacher. He has not left that open to us. He did not intend to.'

In the birth of Jesus, God was doing something special that was way beyond human thought or imagination. The key factor in understanding the birth of Jesus is God's attitude to human sin. God is angry with sin and God's wrath is his anger against those who sin and his determination to punish them. That is not a very popular belief these days, but unquestionably it is what Jesus taught. God, who is completely holy, cannot regard evil and good in the same way. He cannot smile benevolently upon both truth and lies. So God's holiness makes hell as inevitable as his love makes heaven.

God never excuses sin, but in his love and mercy he is willing to pardon and forgive the sinner, but only on his terms. The terms are that the sin must be dealt with and punished, and the sinner must turn to him in repentance and faith.

Jesus had to become a man in order to deal legally and justly with our sin. It was man who had broken God's law and sinned, therefore it had to be man who would pay the penalty for that sin. But there was no man qualified to do this, so God became man in the person of Jesus Christ and did for us what was crucial for our salvation.

Salvation was planned in heaven, but it could not be accomplished in heaven. The punishment of sin must be given to man and the sacrifice that would obtain salvation must be made by man. But all men and women are sinners so there is no one good enough to do this. The only solution was for God to become man 'so that by his death' (Hebrews 2:14) he could purchase salvation for his people. God became man so that as the man Jesus he could die for his people and obtain for them an eternal salvation.

This is why God became man. Jesus is God in the flesh. That is much better than a superstar.

Key Verse/Passage	Hebrews 2:14
Main Point	The C.S. Lewis quote
Key themes	Jesus is God
The 'Story'	Jesus Christ Superstar
Application	How important is all this to our salvation?

49

WHO IS JESUS?

What a tremendous opening John writes for his book. The first verse is thrilling and exciting. The Word, as is clear from verse 14, is Jesus. Jesus was with God. Jesus was God. And all this is true 'in the beginning'. Before creation, before God said, 'Let there be light', Jesus existed with the Father in heaven.

Immediately at the beginning of John's Gospel we are confronted with the uniqueness and exclusiveness of Jesus. He alone brings life and light to a dead, dark world (v. 4). It is in Jesus alone that we can become children of God (v. 12). All through his Gospel John tells us the same thing. His purpose is to exalt the Son of God and put him before us as our only hope and only Savior. In fact, the entire Bible is about the Lord Jesus Christ—who he is, what he has done and what he is going to do.

Jesus is special. John says in verse 14 that the Word became flesh. In the birth of Jesus, God was doing something that was way beyond human thought or imagination. Jesus became man in order to make atonement for man's sin. It was man who had broken God's law and sinned, therefore it had to be a man who would pay the penalty for that sin. But there was no man qualified to do this, so God became man in the person of Jesus Christ and did for us what was crucial for our salvation.

This is what John's Gospel is about. It was written that sinners 'may believe that Jesus is the Christ, the Son of God, and that by believing you may have life in his name' (John 20:31).

John the Baptist had a remarkable ministry and crowds flocked to hear him; but he was only a forerunner. His ministry was to prepare the way for one of whom he said, 'the thongs of whose sandals I am not worthy to untie' (John 1:27). John spoke of Jesus as 'the Lamb of God, who takes away the sin of the world'. He saw Jesus as God's provision to deal with human sin. Clearly the phrase 'Lamb of God' is a special one and must have a meaning that is relevant to the problem of human sin and how God deals with it. What is equally clear is that God always deals with sin justly and mercifully; that is, in wrath and in love. God's justice cannot turn a blind eye to sin.

The only way of dealing with sin in justice is the death of the sinner. So it appears that God's justice leaves no room for mercy. It is because of this that the concept of Christ as the Lamb of God is crucial. It enables the justice of God to be fully satisfied and at the same time the love and mercy of God to be fully operative.

The idea of 'lamb' is taken from the Old Testament sacrificial system where the innocent dies in the place of the guilty. Jesus is the sacrifice who is provided by God to die in the sinner's place. Since the creation of the world the amount of human sin is beyond imagination, but God deems that the death of his Son is sufficient to atone for all that sin.

This speaks volumes for the infinite worth of Jesus. One Jesus is enough to save a multitude no man can number from the consequence of sin. ***Hallelujah, what a Savior!***

Key Verse/Passage	John 1:1
Main Point	The sinlessness of Jesus
Key themes	What has a sinless Jesus got to do with salvation?
The 'Story'	
Application	How real is the sinlessness of Jesus?

50

THE INCARNATION

What does the hymn writer mean when he writes in the great Christmas hymn,

> *Veiled in flesh the Godhead see,*
> *Hail the incarnate deity.*

Incarnation is not a biblical word. It is not found in Scripture, but the teaching is. For instance, John 1:14 says, 'The Word became flesh and lived for a while among us'.

God became man. Not a phantom, not an illusion, but actual flesh and blood. Charles Wesley in another of his Christmas hymns expresses his amazement at this,

> *Our God contracted to a span,*
> *Incomprehensibly made man.*

Wesley's amazement was well founded because this is the most staggering of all Christian doctrines. To quote Wesley again, *He wrapped him in our clay.* This is incomprehensible; it is the most amazing of truths. If this is true then there would be no problem in Jesus walking on water, or feeding 5000 people with a few loaves and fishes. If this is true then miracles and healings become inevitable.

This is almost unbelievable, so the question has to be asked, why did God do it? Why did God become man—exactly like us except for the fact that there was no sin in Jesus, the God Man?

The answer of the Bible is that he had to do it if he was to save sinners. Listen to Hebrews 2:14-18,

14 Since the children have flesh and blood, he too shared in their humanity so that by his death he might destroy him who holds the power of death—that is, the devil—15 and free those who all their lives were held in slavery by their fear of death.
16 For surely it is not angels he helps, but Abraham's descendants. 17 For this reason he had to be made like his brothers in every way, in order that he might become a merciful and faithful high priest in service to God, and that he might make atonement for[j] the sins of the people. 18 Because he himself suffered when he was tempted, he is able to help those who are being tempted.

At Bethlehem God became man. He came into the world in human form. He took human nature and God did this in order to save man. In heaven God would plan salvation but he could not accomplish it there. He had to come to earth as man because it was man who had sinned and therefore man must pay the price of that sin. But this would mean hell for all men and women. God's remedy, to satisfy his own law and justice, was to become man and as the sinless Jesus to die in the place of sinners. This is why God did it. This is why God became man.

The birth of Jesus is not just a nice story for the children, it is the most amazing teaching in the Bible and it is the heart of the gospel.

Key Verse/Passage	Hebrews 2:14-18
Main Point	Why did God become Man?
Key themes	When God became Man it was a real man
The 'Story'	
Application	Hail the incarnate Deity

51

WHY DID JESUS DIE?

Consider carefully the following statements:
The Lord has laid on him the iniquity of us all (Isaiah 53:6).
He himself bore our sins in his body on the tree (1 Peter 2:24).
God made him who had no sin to be sin for us (2 Corinthians 5:21).

Each of them tells us that Jesus died *in our place*. We deserve to die, but he died instead of us. He became our substitute. To use an Old Testament illustration, he became the' scapegoat' (Leviticus 16)—the innocent victim bearing the guilt of others and suffering their just punishment. This was God's plan to make salvation possible for guilty sinners.

On the cross Jesus, bearing our sin and guilt, faced the wrath of God instead of us and paid fully on our behalf the debt we owed to the broken law of God. On the cross our Savior cried, 'My God, my God, why have you forsaken me?' (Matthew 27:46). The holy God forsook his Son because he was our sin-bearer. 'God made him who had no sin to be sin for us' (2 Corinthians 5:21). Jesus was 'stricken by God, smitten by him, and afflicted' (Isaiah 53:4). The Old Testament prophecy of Zechariah 13:7 was being fulfilled: 'Awake, O sword, against my shepherd ...declares the Lord Almighty. Strike the shepherd ...' The sword was the sword of judgment, and in Matthew 26:31 Jesus tells us clearly that this verse speaks of him.

At Calvary, in other words, our Lord made it possible for a holy God to be propitious—or favorably inclined—toward us even though we were sinners and had broken his holy law. God dealt with the problem of sin in the only way that could satisfy his holy justice and enable him to move sin and break the power of Satan in sinners' lives. To think that our efforts could do this is totally to devalue the holiness of God and seriously to underestimate the terribleness of sin in God's sight. We are redeemed, set free from sin's bondage, 'not with perishable things such as silver or gold ...but with the precious blood of Christ, a lamb without blemish or defect' (1 Peter 1:18,19).

The resurrection of Jesus confirms for us that his atoning death was God's plan. It also assures us that the holy God has accepted the atonement made by our Lord on behalf of sinners. Jesus was 'declared with power to be the Son of God by his resurrection from the dead' (Romans 1:4). 'He was delivered over to death for our sins and was raised to life for our justification' (Romans 4:25). 'Death has been swallowed up in victory. Where, O death, is your victory? Where, O death, is your sting? The sting of death is sin, and the power of sin is the law. But thanks be to God! He gives us the victory through our Lord Jesus Christ' (1 Corinthians 15:54-57).

It was the holiness of God that made the atonement necessary, but it was the love of God that made it possible. If God had not loved us, then he would never have sent his Son to die for us.

THE ATONEMENT
The doctrine of atonement is the biblical teaching on the meaning of the death of the Lord Jesus Christ. The atonement is God's answer to human sin, and, as such, is the only effective answer to our sinfulness and guilt. It is crucial therefore that we have a full biblical understanding of what it means.

God's way of salvation did not start in the New Testament when Jesus came into the world. In the Old Testament God ordained certain events that, though important in the lives of the Israelite people at the time, were even more important as vivid illustrations of what Jesus Christ was going to accomplish when he came into the world.

Beware of Rattlesnakes

The Old Testament pictures remind us of two basic facts about the atonement. First, it was planned by God. Peter refers to the death of Jesus as being, 'by God's set purpose and foreknowledge' (Acts 2:23). He later says that Jesus 'was chosen before the creation of the world' to shed his blood for us (1 Peter 1:20). God planned it all to demonstrate his love for us (Romans 5:8).

Secondly, there is nothing hit or miss about our salvation. The death of Jesus was not a tragic mistake but 'God's set purpose'. All the events that led up to Calvary were under God's control. When Pilate said to Jesus that he had power to free him or crucify him, Jesus replied, 'You would have no power over me if it were not given to you from above' (John 19:11). God was in charge at Calvary not Pilate.

Key Verse/Passage	Acts 2:23
Main Point	God planned Calvary
Key themes	The fulfillment of prophecy
The 'Story'	
Application	God's set purpose

52

THE ONLY WAY TO GOD

Jesus says very clearly and plainly in John 14:6 that there is only one way to come to God. "I am the way and the truth and the life. No one comes to the Father except through me." But why only one way?

1 It is God who is providing the way and what God does he does perfectly the first time. If we were doing it we would never get it right and would have to make improvement all the time.
2 For our peace of mind. If there were more than one way we would never be sure that we had got the best way. We have the best way because there is only one way.
3 Because of the nature of salvation. Salvation is from sin but man does not understand his sin. Therefore he cannot understand salvation. Man sees sin as a social blip, a temperamental hic-cup, and not as a direct attack upon the person and integrity of God. Not as a violation of God' law; not as a contradiction to all that God stands for. Sin like this needs an infinite power to overcome it and only God can supply such a power.
4 The cost was so enormous that even God with his infinite resources could not have provided it twice. It took all that God had.

THE WORLD HATES THE ONE WAY.
A world that can tolerate just about anything—homosexuality, lesbianism, abortion; cannot tolerate one way to God. Of all things about the Christian faith what the world hates most is teaching about the uniqueness and exclusiveness of Jesus.

Given the religious thought of today this truth is unacceptable to many. They regard it as bigoted and a failure to recognize the worth of religions other than Christianity. The prevailing thought is that everyone is entitled to his opinion and that one religious opinion is as good as the next. A more unreasonable and absurd attitude it would be difficult to find. How can several diametrically-opposed teachings on the way to God all be right? It is like a man in Edinburgh asking the way to London and being given the conflicting instructions to take a plane and fly west, take a boat and go east, take a train and go south. If he has any sense he will know that all the answers cannot be right. If he takes the trouble to look at a map he will be able to decide which piece of advice he should follow.

Accepting the truth that Jesus is the only way to God is not intolerant bigotry: it is simply believing the teaching God has given us in his Word. There Jesus said, 'I am the way and the truth and the life. No one comes to the Father except through me' (John 14:6).

Peter said, 'Salvation is found in no one else, for there is no other name under heaven given to men by which we must be saved' (Acts 4:12).

Paul said, 'For there is one God and one mediator between God and men, the man Christ Jesus' (1 Timothy 2:5).

Nothing is more clearly stated in the Bible. The above quotes can bear no interpretation other than that Jesus is the only way to God.

NO OTHER WAY

In John 14:6, the verse quoted above, Jesus is not saying that he is one of many ways to God but that he is the *only way*. There is a uniqueness and exclusiveness about Jesus when it comes to the matter of our salvation. There is a triple claim in that verse which is quite amazing. Jesus is *the* way and *the* truth and *the* life. There is no alternative to him and the second part of the verse confirms this: 'No one comes to the Father except through me.'

Why is Jesus so adamant that he is the only way to God? The stand he is taking leaves him either totally deluded or totally correct. There is no room for half measure. Either Jesus is deluded and we can safely ignore him, or he is right and therefore it would be the greatest possible folly to ignore him. Our eternal destiny hangs upon this; so do we believe that Jesus is the only way to God?

WHAT ALTERNATIVE DO YOU HAVE?
Because of its hatred of one-way Christianity the world has spent the past 2000 years looking for an alternative to Jesus. Self-effort, morality, all sorts of variations of Christianity, and every conceivable alternative religion have been put forward. All this has been useless in man's search for God so at last the final answer has been found—there is no God, people say so therefore we don't need a way to God.

But when man has made all his pronouncements about life and death, and eternity, there still remains the great unalterable fact of GOD. And there is still only one way to know this God. There is no alternative to Jesus. That is where you are now. It is either Jesus or Hell. What a choice! In all the choices you have to make in life none is so clear and obvious as this.

As this little book draws to a close, let me invite you one last time to place all your hopes, all your fears, all your cares, all your sins, and all your trust in Jesus Christ the Lord.

Key Verse/Passage	John 14:6
Main Point	There is no alternative to Jesus
Key themes	Why does the world hate the one way?
The 'Story'	
Application	Consider the message of 1 Timothy 2:5

OTHER SOLID GROUND TITLES

In addition to *Beware of Rattlesnakes,* Solid Ground Christian Books is honored to offer many other titles for the young, many for the first time in more than a century:

THE MOTHER AT HOME by John S.C. Abbott
THE CHILD AT HOME by John S.C. Abbott
THE FAMILY AT HOME by Gorham Abbott
THE PUBLICATIONS OF THE AMERICAN TRACT SOCIETY
BIBLE PROMISES: *Sermons for Children* by Richard Newton
BIBLE WARNINGS: *Sermons for Children* by Richard Newton
BIBLE ANIMALS: *Lessons for the Children* by Richard Newton
BIBLE JEWELS: *Lessons for the Children* by Richard Newton
THE KING'S HIGHWAY: *10 Commandments for the Young* by Richard Newton
HEROES OF THE REFORMATION by Richard Newton
HEROES OF THE EARLY CHURCH by Richard Newton
SAFE COMPASS AND HOW IT POINTS by Richard Newton
RAYS FROM THE SON OF RIGHTEOUSNESS by Richard Newton
THE LIFE OF JESUS CHRIST FOR THE YOUNG by Richard Newton
FEED MY LAMBS: *Lectures to Children on Vital Subjects* by John Todd
TRUTH MADE SIMPLE: *Attributes of God to Children* by John Todd
THE STILL HOUR: *Communion with God in Prayer* by Austin Phelps
THE SECRET OF COMMUNION WITH GOD by Matthew Henry
OPENING SCRIPTURE: *Hermeneutical Manual* by Patrick Fairbairn
THE ASSURANCE OF FAITH *by Louis Berkhof*
THE PASTOR IN THE SICK ROOM *by John D. Wells*
THE POWER OF GOD UNTO SALVATION *by B.B. Warfield*
THE LORD OF GLORY *by B.B. Warfield*
SERMONS TO THE NATURAL MAN *by W.G.T. Shedd*
SERMONS TO THE SPIRITUAL MAN *by W.G.T. Shedd*
A PASTOR'S SKETCHES 1 & 2 *by Ichabod S. Spencer*
IMAGO CHRISTI: *The Example of Jesus Christ by James Stalker*
THE SHORTER CATECHISM ILLUSTRATED *by John Whitecross*
THE CHURCH MEMBER'S GUIDE *by John Angell James*
THE SUNDAY SCHOOL TEACHER'S GUIDE *by John A. James*
CHRIST IN SONG: *Hymns of Immanuel from All Ages by Philip Schaff*
COME YE APART: *Daily Words from the Four Gospels by J.R. Miller*
DEVOTIONAL LIFE OF THE S.S. TEACHER *by J.R. Miller*

Call us 205-443-0311
Send us an e-mail at mike.sgcb@gmail.com
Visit us on line at www.solid-ground-books.com

CPSIA information can be obtained at www.ICGtesting.com
Printed in the USA
LVOW10s0327030114

367805LV00001B/2/P